D0463715

Praise for *The Christian Lover*

The Christian Lover is both insightful and inspirational. Your heart will be touched as you gain a brief glimpse into the love shared by these heroes of the faith. Be prepared for the unexpected. The passions of these couples will surprise you, but you will not be disappointed.

—DR. DANIEL L. AKIN
President
Southeastern Baptist Theological Seminary
Wake Forest, N.C.

Michael Haykin is to be congratulated for compiling this remarkable collection of beautiful love letters from some of the most significant and faithful Christian leaders in the history of the church. These inspiring letters, along with the informative introductions, will provide great strength and guidance for Christian couples at a time when the institution of marriage is facing challenges from numerous directions. I heartily commend this wonderful volume.

—DR. DAVID S. DOCKERY
President
Union University
Jackson, Tenn.

In an era in which love is equated with the adolescent, hormonal romance of popular music, Michael Haykin serves the church with a decidedly different vision of Christian love. *The Christian Lover* demonstrates a deep, authentic view of Christ-centered love.

—Dr. Russell D. Moore
Dean of the School of Theology
The Southern Baptist Theological Seminary
Louisville, Ky.

The Christian Lover portrays some of our most revered historical personalities as men of deep marital love. Haykin's work enhances (rather than diminishes) the pictures we have of them as towering scholars, faithful pastors, pioneering missionaries, and bold martyrs. This epistolary anthology of the Puritan and Reformed divines' marital love may serve as a great buttress to the continued testimony of the goodness of marriage as the Creator's provision for a companionship of joy in the highest order. May all in the church who read these accounts of love be awakened to the passionate pursuit of the lifelong, unbreakable, satisfying relationship every marriage should be. My heart was stirred more with each letter.

—Rev. Eric C. Redmond
Pastor
Hillcrest Baptist Church
Temple Hills, Md.

C. S. Lewis once made the striking statement that "Christianity has glorified marriage than any other religion: and nearly all the greatest love poetry in the world has been produced by Christians." *The Christian Lover* provides a double lens by which to view the Christian ideal of wedded romantic love. One is the author's selection of a dozen Christian couples and their life stories. The other is a sampling of letters these men and women wrote, from which we can catch glimpses of what a romantic relationship between husband and wife can be—anytime, anywhere.

—DR. LELAND RYKEN
Professor of English
Wheaton College
Wheaton, Ill.

Michael Haykin never ceases to surprise with his gift for producing unusual books on neglected aspects of church history. Here he gives his readers insights into the love lives of some of the great saints of the past, bringing out their humanity in touching and unique ways. An unusual book, certainly, but well worth reading.

—DR. CARL R. TRUEMAN
Professor of historical theology and church history
Westminster Theological Seminary
Philadelphia, Pa.

The

CHRISTIAN
LOVER

The

CHRISTIAN
LOVER

THE SWEETNESS OF LOVE AND MARRIAGE
IN THE LETTERS OF BELIEVERS

MICHAEL A.G. HAYKIN
with VICTORIA J. HAYKIN

R
Reformation Trust
PUBLISHING

A DIVISION OF LIGONIER MINISTRIES · ORLANDO, FLORIDA

The Christian Lover: *The Sweetness of Love and Marriage
in the Letters of Believers*

© 2009 by Michael A. G. Haykin
Published by Reformation Trust Publishing
a division of Ligonier Ministries
400 Technology Park, Lake Mary, FL 32746
www.ligonier.org www.reformationtrust.com

Printed in the United States of America

All rights reserved. No part of this publication may be reproduced, stored in
a retrieval system, or transmitted in any form or by any means—electronic,
mechanical, photocopy, recording, or otherwise—without the prior written
permission of the publisher, Reformation Trust. The only exception is brief
quotations in printed reviews.

Cover design: Gearbox Studios
Interior design and typeset: Katherine Lloyd, The DESK

Library of Congress Cataloging-in-Publication Data

Haykin, Michael A. G.
  The Christian lover : the sweetness of love and marriage in the letters of
believers / by Michael A.G. Haykin.
      p. cm.
  Includes bibliographical references.
  ISBN 978-1-56769-111-5
  1. Marriage--Religious aspects--Christianity. 2. Love-letters. I. Title.
  BV835.H3795 2009
  261.8'3581--dc22

                                    2008044024

To the love of my life, Alison,
to whom it has been ever my privilege
and my delight to have written letters from time to time

Contents

INTRODUCTION

"How greatly are we inclined to the other sex," Jonathan Edwards (1703–1758) observed in the spring of 1725 after he had met Sarah Pierpont (1710–1758), whom he would marry just over two years later.[1] This observation serves as a concise summary of God's divine purpose in creating humanity male and female. At the heart of marriage, as conceived by God in the primal state, is the intention that the husband delight in and passionately love his wife, and vice versa.

Another eighteenth-century author, the London Baptist Samuel Stennett (1727–1795), rightly maintained that when God declared in Genesis 2:18 that He would make a helpmeet for the man after no fit companion was found for him among the animals, it was as if God had said, "It is fit that man whom I have made for society, should have one for his companion, with whom he may intimately converse, and who may assist him in the duties and be a sharer with him in the joys of life."

This meant, from Stennett's perspective, that "the woman was created, and given to man in marriage, not merely for the purpose of propagating the species, but for that of promoting his and her own felicity." Undergirding their marriage was to be an "unextinguishable flame" of love, "a flame which the endearing intercourses of virtuous friendship will daily fan, and the most tempestuous storms of worldly adversity will not be able to put out," for the relationship of the two is to be "very intimate."[2]

A cursory study of the history of love and marriage within Christian circles will reveal, however, that this divine ideal has not always been heeded and, indeed, sometimes has been rejected.

SOME PATRISTIC PERSPECTIVES

For instance, the fourth-century Bible scholar, Jerome (d. 420), who was responsible for the Latin translation of the Bible known as the Vulgate, vigorously defended the view that celibacy was a vastly superior state to marriage, seeing it as far more virtuous and much more pleasing to God. In Jerome's thinking, those who were closest to God in the historical narrative recorded in the Scriptures were all celibate. In fact, Jerome argued, sexual relations between spouses were a distinct obstacle to leading a life devoted to the pursuit of genuine spirituality.[3]

Augustine (354–430), another Latin-speaking theologian from the same era, whose thought provided the foundation for much of the thinking of the Middle Ages, similarly maintained that the celibate individual who devotes himself or herself to Christ is like the angels who do not marry. Celibate individuals, he said, experience a foretaste of heaven, for in heaven there is no marriage.[4] Why, then, did God ordain marriage? In Augustine's eyes, it was primarily for the procreation of children. Commenting on Genesis 2, Augustine declared that Eve would have been no use to Adam if she had not been able to bear children.

What, then, of the biblical idea, found in this very chapter of Genesis, that the woman was made to be a delightful companion to the man, a source of comfort and strength? And what of the man as such a companion for the woman? These ideas receive scant attention in the theology of Augustine.[5] Instead, he argues that God instituted marriage for three basic reasons:

- for the sake of fidelity, that is, the avoidance of illicit sex;
- for the purpose of procreation;
- as a symbol of the unity of those who would inherit the heavenly Jerusalem.[6]

With slight differences of emphasis, these positions of Jerome and Augustine were largely embraced by the various Roman Catholic authors of the Middle Ages.

One example must suffice. It comes from the commentary of Bede (ca. 673–735) on 1 Peter 3:7:

Sexual intercourse is a barrier to prayer. . . . This means that whenever I have intercourse I cannot pray. But if we are supposed to pray without ceasing, as Paul also said, it is obvious that I can never have sexual intercourse, because if I do so I shall have to interrupt my prayers.[7]

THE REDISCOVERY OF CHRISTIAN MARRIAGE

For many in Western Europe, the Reformation in the sixteenth century was not only a rediscovery of the heart of the gospel and the way of salvation, long hidden under centuries of superstition and theological error, but a recovery of a fully biblical view of marriage. After the death of his wife Idelette in March 1549, John Calvin (1509–1564), for example, wrote to his fellow Reformer, Pierre Viret (1511–1571): "I am deprived of my excellent life companion, who, if misfortune had come, would have been my willing companion not only in exile and sorrow, but even in death."[8] This simple statement from one of the central figures in the Reformation, who was normally very discreet about his personal feelings, reveals a view of marriage poles apart from that of medieval Roman Catholicism. For the Reformers and those who followed in their steps—such as the Puritans of the seventeenth century and the evangelicals of the eighteenth and nineteenth centuries—marriage had an innate excellence, was vital for the development of Christian affection and friendship, and was one of God's major means for developing Christian character and spiritual maturity.

Consider the English Puritans, who have been wrongly regarded as utter prudes when it comes to the joys and delights of marriage, especially those dealing with the experience of sex.[9] As J. I. Packer puts it, they gave marriage "such strength, substance, and solidity as to warrant the verdict that . . . under God . . . they were creators of the English Christian marriage."[10] Like the Reformers, the Puritans strongly opposed clerical celibacy and affirmed that marriage is as intrinsically good as virginity, even hinting that it might be better. Thomas Adams (fl. 1612–1653), a renowned Puritan preacher, declared, "There is no such fountain of comfort on earth, as marriage."[11] Similarly, the Elizabethan Puritan author Robert Cleaver stated, "There can be no greater society or company, than is between a man and his wife."[12] And a later Puritan preacher and author, George Swinnock (1627–1673), said of husband and wife, "They are partners in the nearest degree imaginable."[13] The New England Puritan Thomas Hooker (ca. 1586–1647) put it beautifully when he wrote, "The man whose heart is endeared to the woman he loves, he dreams of her in the night, hath her in his eye and apprehension when he awakes, museth on her as he sits at table, walks with her when he travels and parlies with her in each place where he comes."[14] In another context, Hooker noted of husband and wife, "She lies in his bosom, and his heart trusts in her, which forceth all to confess, that the stream of his affection, like a mighty current, runs with full tide and strength."[15] It was thus not fortuitous that when the writers of that quintessential Puritan text, the Westminster Confession of Faith, listed the reasons for marriage, they placed companionship first. "Marriage was ordained," chapter 25.2 declares, "for the mutual help of husband and wife, for the increase of mankind with a legitimate issue, and of the Church with an holy seed; and for preventing uncleanness."[16]

As Packer notes, Puritan preachers and authors are regularly "found pulling out the stops to proclaim the supreme blessing of togetherness in marriage."[17] They rightly saw that this was a central emphasis of scriptural passages that address the purpose of marriage: for instance, Richard Baxter (1615–1691) stated:

> It is a mercy to have a faithful friend, that loveth you entirely, and is as true to you as yourself, to whom you may open your mind and communicate your affairs, and who would be ready to strengthen you, and divide the cares of your affairs and family with you, and help you to bear your burdens, and comfort you in your sorrows, and be the daily companion of your lives, and partaker of your joys and sorrows. And it is a mercy to have so near a friend to be a helper to your soul; to join with you in prayer and other holy exercises; to watch over you and tell you of your sins and dangers, and to stir up in you the grace of God, and remember to you of the life to come, and cheerfully accompany you in the ways of holiness.[18]

CELEBRATING CHRISTIAN LOVE AND MARRIAGE

With the significant increase of divorce in Western societies during the past fifty years and the call for the legal recognition of gay and lesbian unions, there is little doubt that marriage in general is under heavy attack in our day. Neither are Christian marriages immune. Divorce has become a frequent option after serious marital discord for Christians, and homosexuality has not left Christian marriages unravaged. This small anthology grows out of the conviction that the Reformers and the Puritans were right on the big issues about love and marriage, and that thinking about the past with regard to this issue and reading expressions of love from the past can be a helpful way of responding to the frangibility of Christian marriage in our day.

Anthologies such as this one are inevitably somewhat eclectic and reflect personal preferences. The final letter, for example, from Helmuth James von Moltke (1907–1945) to his wife Freya (1911–), I first read in the 1970s, and it deeply impressed me as to how a Christian can live in one of the most heinous of states known to human history. Its power to move and inspire me has not diminished over the decades. I first encountered the love letters of Samuel Pearce (1766–1799) at the end of the 1980s, and they have been a regular part of my reading ever since. I am, in fact, currently working on two literary projects dealing with Pearce's life. I have always regarded Calvin's letters about his wife's death as providing an excellent window into his

personality, which was anything but dour, but deeply passionate. I encountered most of the other letters as a result of preparing to write this book, but the choice of authors reflects some
longtime favorites, such as the ever-colorful Martin Luther,
that winsome author Philip Doddridge, the fascinating Baptist
Benjamin Beddome, and Martyn Lloyd-Jones, ever a mentor
of my Christian pilgrimage.

While most of the chapters contain only a couple of letters apiece, I have included around four or five letters apiece of
Philip and Mercy Doddridge and Thomas and Sally Charles.
In part, this is because of my interest in them as couples. I am
confident, though, that what I find attractive in them will draw
others to be interested readers of their letters.

Letters of other figures could have been included in this
work, but hopefully the letters I have selected reveal the full
range of the experience of Christian marriage, from the first
flush of love to the ups and downs of married life to the experience of grief when one of the spouses goes to be with the Lord
of glory. All in all, they are a reminder of what an awesome
experience and privilege love for another human being is, and
that, from the Christian standpoint, married love at its best is
a foretaste of eternal bliss. It was not without reason that Paul
in Ephesians 5 compared the love of the Lord Jesus for His
church to the love of the husband for his wife.

Some of the letters included in this anthology have been

lightly edited: punctuation, capitalization, and paragraph divisions have been made amenable to modern reading habits.

———

Anyone who writes a book like this incurs debts. First of all, I am deeply indebted to my daughter, Victoria J. Haykin, who worked as my research assistant for the summer of 2008 and typed out most of the letters in this anthology. She also did some of the basic research for the mini-biographical introductions to each couple. Then, I am thankful to Jason Fowler, the Southern Baptist Theological Seminary archivist, and to Chris Dewease, his assistant, for help with the Broadus letters. A number of years ago, Stephen Pickles of Oxford, who has been researching the life of Anne Steele, drew my attention to Broome's discovery of the letter of Benjamin Beddome to Miss Steele. Dr. Tom Nettles suggested the inclusion of the letters of Adoniram Judson, advice I have happily followed. Judson's letter to his first wife's father seeking his permission to marry his daughter has to be unique indeed. Dr. Wyn James of Cardiff University selected and transcribed all of the Charles letters, though I added the annotation. Marylynn Rouse of Stratford-upon-Avon, England, expert in all things Newtonian (that is, John Newton), identified a Newton quote in one of Thomas Charles' letters and provided helpful detail about it. Dr. Robert Strivens of London Theological Seminary, England, helped with regard to the Doddridge letters, for which I had relied on the notoriously deficient nineteenth-century edition of Doddridge's correspondence.

Finally, I have dedicated this anthology to my wife, Alison: for me, the dearest of women.

Notes

1 Cited in George M. Marsden, *A Short Life of Jonathan Edwards* (Grand Rapids/Cambridge, U.K.: Eerdmans, 2008), 31.

2 Samuel Stennett, *Discourses on Domestick Duties* (London, 1783), 144–145, 174, 177.

3 J. N. D. Kelly, *Jerome: His Life, Writings, and Controversies* (New York: Harper & Row, 1975), 183, 187.

4 James A. Mohler, *Late Have I Loved You: An Interpretation of Saint Augustine on Human and Divine Relationships* (New York: New City Press, 1991), 71.

5 Edmund Leites, "The Duty to Desire: Love, Friendship, and Sexuality in Some Puritan Theories of Marriage," *Journal of Social History*, 15 (1981–1982), 384.

6 Mohler, *Late Have I Loved You*, 68.

7 *James, 1–2 Peter, 1–3 John, Jude*, ed. Gerald Bray (*Ancient Christian Commentary on Scripture: New Testament*, vol. 11; Downers Grove, Ill.: InterVarsity, 2000), 100.

8 Cited in Richard Stauffer, *The Humanness of John Calvin*, trans. George H. Shriver (Nashville: Abingdon, 1971), 45.

9 There are numerous studies of this fact, but see especially two, the first from a secular commentator, the second by a Christian author: Morton M. Hunt, "The Impuritans," in his *The Natural History of Love* (New York: Alfred A. Knopf, 1959), 215–252, and Joel R. Beeke, "The Puritan Marriage," in his *Living for God's Glory: An Introduction to Calvinism* (Orlando, Fla.: Reformation Trust Publishing, 2008), 317–332.

10 J. I. Packer, "Marriage and Family in Puritan Thought," in his *A Quest for Godliness: The Puritan Vision of the Christian Life* (Wheaton, Ill.: Crossway,

1990), 259–260.

11 Cited in C. H. George and K. George, *The Protestant Mind of the English Reformation 1570–1640* (Princeton: Princeton University Press, 1961), 268.

12 Cited in Margo Todd, *Christian Humanism and the Puritan Social Order* (Cambridge: Cambridge University Press, 1987), 100. For further discussion, see Daniel Doriani, "The Puritans, Sex, and Pleasure," *Westminster Theological Journal*, 53 (1991), 128–129, and Leland Ryken, *Worldly Saints: The Puritans as They Really Were* (Grand Rapids: Zondervan, 1986), 41–42.

13 Cited in Michael Parsons, "Marriage under Threat in the Writing of George Swinnock," *Scottish Bulletin of Evangelical Theology*, 20, No.1 (Spring 2002), 42, n47.

14 Thomas Hooker, *The Application of Redemption* (London: Peter Cole, 1659), 137. For this quote, I am indebted to Beeke, "The Puritan Marriage," in his *Living for God's Glory*, 325.

15 Thomas Hooker, *A Comment Upon Christ's Last Prayer* (London: Peter Cole, 1656), 187. For this quote, I am indebted to Beeke, "The Puritan Marriage," in his *Living for God's Glory*, 325.

16 On the significance of the order of reasons given for the institution of marriage, see Packer, *A Quest for Godliness*, 261–262. See also Todd, *Christian Humanism and the Puritan Social Order*, 99–100.

17 Packer, *A Quest for Godliness*, 262.

18 Richard Baxter, *A Christian Directory; or, A Sum of Practical Theology, and Cases of Conscience*, II.1 (*The Practical Works of the Rev. Richard Baxter* [London: James Duncan, 1830], IV, 30).

"Love is a talkative passion."

—Bishop Thomas Wilson[1]

Note

1   This quote from Thomas Wilson (1663–1755), Anglican bishop of Sodor and Man, often appears in anthologies of love letters, though the full statement actually reads thus: "Love is a talkative passion, and yet the divine lover is backward to talk of the very delight of his soul." (*Sacra privata* in *The Works of the Right Reverend Father in God, Thomas Wilson, D.D.* [Oxford: John Henry Parker, 1860], V, 194).

Chapter One

MARTIN & KATHARINA LUTHER

artin Luther (1483–1546) played a vital role in the recovery of the biblical doctrine of salvation at the time of the sixteenth-century Reformation. As noted in the introduction, though, the Reformation also involved a rediscovery of Christian marriage. Just as Luther's experience of conversion proved to be paradigmatic for many in sixteenth-century Europe for the rediscovery of true Christian salvation, so his experience of wedlock became paradigmatic for the recovery of the biblical view of marriage.

At Easter 1523, Luther arranged for the escape of twelve Cistercian nuns in empty barrels from a nearby Roman Catholic nunnery. Luther found himself acting as a matchmaker for most of these women over the course of the next two years, until all were married save one, Katharina von Bora (1499–1552). She apparently had her heart set on marrying Luther. When they eventually did marry, in June 1525, Luther had a strange trio of reasons for his entry into the state of matrimony: "to please his father, to spite the Pope and the Devil, and to seal his witness before his martyrdom"![1] Those were not the most romantic of reasons for marrying, but Martin and Katie came to have a fabulous marriage. One gets a glimpse of the joy they found in each other when he stated, "I give more credit to Katherine than to Christ, who has done so much more for me."[2]

In the two letters of Luther that follow, written in the year of his death, one sees Luther's keen sense of humor, but also his awareness of the responsibility of a married man or woman to pray for his or her spouse. Also evident is the responsibility to encourage one's spouse in the faith.

Martin Luther to Katharina Luther,
Halle, January 25, 1546

> *Martin Luther to my kind and dear Katie Luther,*
> *a brewer and a judge at the pig market at Wittenberg[3]*
> *Grace and Peace in the Lord! Dear Katie! Today at eight*
> *we drove away from Halle, yet did not get to Eisleben, but*
> *returned to Halle again by nine. For a huge female Anabaptist*

met us with waves of water and great floating pieces of ice; she threatened to baptize us again, and has covered the [whole] countryside.[4] But we are also unable to return because of the Mulde [River] at Bitterfeld, and are forced to stay captive here at Halle between the waters—not that we are thirsty to drink of them. Instead we take good beer from Torgau and good wine from the Rhine, with which we refresh and comfort ourselves in the meantime, hoping that the rage of the Saale [River] may wear itself out today. For since the ferryman and the people themselves were of little courage [to try to cross], we did not want to go into the water and tempt God. For the devil is angry at us, and he lives in the water. Foresight is better than hindsight, and there is no need for us to prepare a fool's delight for the pope and his hangers-on. I did not think that the Saale could create such a flood and rumble over the stones and everything in such a way.

No more for now. You people pray for us, and be good. I am sure that, if you were here, you too would have advised us to proceed in this way; [so,] you see, at least once we are following your advice. With this I commend you to God. Amen. . . .

—Martin Luther. Doctor

Martin Luther to Katharina Luther,
[Eisleben,] February 10, 1546

Martin Luther to the holy lady, full of worries,
Mrs. Katharina, doctor, the lady of Zölsdorf, at Wittenberg,
my gracious, dear mistress of the house[5]

    Grace and peace in Christ! Most holy Mrs. Doctor! I thank
you very kindly for your great worry which robs you of sleep.
Since the date that you [started to] worry about me, the fire
in my quarters, right outside the room, tried to devour me;
and yesterday, no doubt because of the strength of your wor-
ries, a stone almost fell on my head and nearly squashed me as
in a mouse trap. For in our secret chamber[6] mortar has been
falling down for about two days; we called in some people who
[merely] touched the stone with two fingers and it fell down. The
stone was as big as a long pillow and as wide as a large hand; it
intended to repay you for your holy worries, had the dear angels
not protected [me]. [Now] I worry that if you do not stop
worrying the earth will finally swallow us up and all the ele-
ments will chase us. Is this the way you learned the Catechism
and the faith? Pray, and let God worry. You have certainly not
been commanded to worry about me or yourself. "Cast your
burden on the Lord, and he will sustain you," as is written in
Psalm 55[:22] and many more passages. . . .

                                 Your Holiness' willing servant,
                                        Martin Luther

Notes

1 Roland Bainton, *Here I Stand: A Life of Martin Luther* (New York/Nashville: Abingdon, 1950), 288.

2 Cited in ibid., 293. For Luther's views on marriage, see ibid., 298–302, and Michael Parsons, *Reformation Marriage: The Husband and Wife Relationship in the Theology of Luther and Calvin* (Edinburgh: Rutherford House, 2005), 103–212.

3 From *Luther's Works: Vol. 50: Letters III*, ed. and trans. Gottfried G. Krodel (Philadelphia: Fortress, 1975), 286–287. Used by permission. Luther literally addressed his wife as "a brewress and she-judge." The reference to Katharina being a judge was probably a reference to her ability at running their home. See *Luther's Works: Vol. 50: Letters III*, 286, n10.

4 Luther is referring to a flood of water when a sudden thaw caused the Saale River to overflow its banks.

5 *Luther's Works: Vol. 50: Letters III*, 305–306. Used by permission. Zölsdorf was a country estate that Luther purchased in the spring of 1540. See *Luther's Works: Vol. 50: Letters III*, 208, n13.

6 That is, the toilet.

Chapter Two

JOHN & IDELETTE CALVIN

*I*f Martin Luther was the pioneer of the Reformation, his younger contemporary, John Calvin (1509–1563), should be regarded as the Reformation's systematic theologian. For nearly all of his ministry, from 1536 till his death in 1564, Calvin was in exile in Francophone Geneva. These years in Geneva were interrupted, though, by a period spent in Strasbourg from 1538 to 1541, and it was during that period that Calvin married.

At the urging of a number of friends, including his close colleague Guillaume Farel (1489–1565), Calvin had drawn up a list of the attributes he sought in a wife. He was not really concerned with physical beauty, he told Farel on one occasion. Instead, he was looking for a woman who was chaste, sober-minded, prudent, patient, and able "to take care of my health."[1] Farel told him that he knew just the woman, but it didn't work out. Then a woman from the upper class was proposed. But she couldn't speak French, about which Calvin was not at all happy. Calvin was also afraid that her social status might be an inducement to pride. Calvin's brother Antoine (d. 1573), though, was keen about the marriage. So Calvin agreed to consider marriage as long as the woman promised to learn French. This was at the beginning of 1540.[2] But by late March of that year, Calvin was saying that he would never think of marrying her "unless the Lord had entirely bereft me of my wits."[3]

By August, however, he had met and married another woman, a widow by the name of Idelette de Bure (ca. 1499–1549) who had two children. Her first husband, Jean Stordeur (d. 1540), had been an Anabaptist leader, who, through discussing theology with Calvin, had become convinced of the Reformed position.

Calvin did not say a lot about his wife in his letters during their eight and a half years of marriage (she died in March 1549, having suffered from ill health for a number of years), but two statements reveal how close they were.[4] For example, during the spring of 1541, before he returned to Geneva, Calvin was with his wife in Strasbourg. A plague was raging in the city, and Calvin decided to stay in Strasbourg but send his wife away for her safety. He wrote to Farel that "day and night my wife has been constantly in my thoughts, in need of advice now that she is separated from her husband."[5] A second state-ment appears in a letter written after the death of their one son, Jacques, who died soon after his premature birth in 1542. "The Lord," Calvin wrote to another close friend, Pierre Viret (1511–1571), "has certainly inflicted a severe and bitter wound in the death of our baby son. But he is himself a Father and knows best what is good for his children."[6]

In the two letters that follow, Calvin gives details of Ide-lette's death to Viret and Farel. His intense grief speaks to his deep love for her. And one sees Calvin's tenderness toward his wife as he tells of his steps to relieve any anxieties she may have had about the future of her children after her death. Such kindness is a model for spouses.

John Calvin to Pierre Viret [7]
April 7, 1549

Although the death of my wife has been exceedingly painful to me, yet I subdue my grief as well as I can. Friends, also, are earnest in their duty to me. It might be wished, indeed, that they could profit me and themselves more; yet one can scarcely say how much I am supported by their attentions. But you know well enough how tender, or rather soft, my mind is. Had not a powerful self-control, therefore, been vouchsafed to me, I could not have borne up so long. And truly mine is no common source of grief. I have been bereaved of the best companion of my life, of one who, had it been so ordered, would not only have been the willing sharer of my indigence, but even of my death. During her life she was the faithful helper of my ministry. From her I never experienced the slightest hindrance. She was never troublesome to me throughout the entire course of her illness; she was more anxious about her children than about herself. As I feared these private cares might annoy her to no purpose, I took occasion, on the third day before her death, to mention that I would not fail in discharging my duty to her children. Taking up the matter immediately, she said, "I have already committed them to God." When I said that was not to prevent me from caring for them, she replied, "I know you will not neglect what you know has been committed to God."

John Calvin to Guillaume Farel [8]
Geneva, April 11, 1549

Intelligence of my wife's death has perhaps reached you before now. I do what I can to keep myself from being overwhelmed with grief. My friends also leave nothing undone that may administer relief to my mental suffering. When your brother left, her life was all but despaired of. When the brethren were assembled on Tuesday, they thought it best that we should join together in prayer. This was done. When Abel, in the name of the rest, exhorted her to faith and patience, she briefly (for she was now greatly worn) stated her frame of mind. I afterwards added an exhortation, which seemed to me appropriate to the occasion. And then, as she had made no allusion to her children, I, fearing that, restrained by modesty, she might be feeling an anxiety concerning them, which would cause her greater suffering than the disease itself, declared in the presence of the brethren, that I should henceforth care for them as if they were my own. She replied, "I have already committed them to the Lord." When I replied, that that was not to hinder me from doing my duty, she immediately answered, "If the Lord shall care for them, I know they will be commended to you." Her magnanimity was so great, that she seemed to have already left the world.

About the sixth hour of the day, on which she yielded up her soul to the Lord, our brother Bourgouin[9] addressed some pious words to her, and while he was doing so, she spoke aloud, so that all saw that her heart was raised far above the world. For these were her words: "O glorious resurrection! O God of Abraham, and of all our fathers, in thee have the faithful trusted during so many past ages, and none of them have trusted in vain. I also will hope." These short sentences were rather ejaculated than distinctly spoken. This did not come from the suggestion of others, but from her own reflections, so that she made it obvious in few words what were her own meditations.

I had to go out at six o'clock. Having been removed to another apartment after seven, she immediately began to decline. When she felt her voice suddenly failing her, she said: "Let us pray: let us pray. All pray for me." I had now returned. She was unable to

speak, and her mind seemed to be troubled. I, having spoken a few
words about the love of Christ, the hope of eternal life, concern-
ing our married life, and her departure, engaged in prayer. In full
possession of her mind, she both heard the prayer, and attended
to it. Before eight she expired, so calmly, that those present could
scarcely distinguish between her life and her death. I at present
control my sorrow so that my duties may not be interfered with. . . .

Adieu, brother, and very excellent friend. May the Lord
Jesus strengthen you by his Spirit; and may he support me also
under this heavy affliction, which would certainly overcome me
had not he, who raises up the prostrate, strengthens the weak,
and refreshes the weary, stretched forth his hand from heaven to
me. Salute all the brethren and your whole family.

—Yours,
John Calvin

Notes

1 T. H. L. Parker, *John Calvin: A Biography* (Philadelphia: Westminster, 1975), 71.

2 Ibid, 71–72.

3 Cited in ibid., 72.

4 T. H. L. Parker, *Portrait of Calvin* (London: SCM Press, 1954), 70–71.

5 Cited in ibid., 71.

6 Cited in ibid.

7 From *Letters of John Calvin*, compiled by Jules Bonnet (1858 ed.; repr. New York: Burt Franklin, 1972), II, 217–219.

8 From ibid., 216–217.

9 François Bourgouin was one of the elders in the Geneva church.

Chapter Three

JOHN & LUCY HUTCHINSON

*J*ohn Hutchinson (1615–1664) was the Puritan military commander of Nottingham during the British Civil Wars (1642–1651), a role so significant he was one of the judges who signed the death warrant of Charles I in 1649. In 1638, he married Lady Lucy Apsley (1620–?)[1], a daughter of the lieutenant of the Tower of London, Sir Allen Apsley. Lucy's father had spared no expense on her education. She had been taught both French and Latin, and her writings indicate a fair degree of competency in both classical Greek and Hebrew. During her early married years she translated some of the poetry of the Roman materialist Lucretius (ca. 99–55 BC) into verse, though, later, as she became more committed as a Christian, she was ashamed of having translated the pagan author and refused to allow her translation to be published. She also authored a "militantly Trinitarian and Calvinist" epic poem based on Genesis, *Order and Disorder*, only recently published in its entirety.[2]

After the Restoration of the monarchy in 1660, John Hutchinson, unlike other regicides, escaped with his life, partly because of the influence of royalists in his wife's family and partly because of his own expressions of remorse for having participated in the trial and execution of Charles I. In 1663, however, he was arrested on suspicion of plotting against the government and imprisoned in Sandown Castle, Kent. Lucy later noted that the chamber in which he was imprisoned was so "unwholesome and damp" that even in the summer all of Hutchinson's leather goods would be "all covered over with mould,—wipe them as clean as you could one morning, by the next day they would be mouldy again."[3] Lucy visited him regularly during this time of imprisonment, but she was not with him when he died of a fever, presumably contracted from the damp conditions in which he was confined.

Determined to vindicate her husband's memory, Lucy drew up a memoir of her husband initially for their children. It was completed in 1671, after seven years of labor, though, because of its political reflections, it was not published till 1806. It preserves a beautiful picture of the life and passion of a Puritan marriage. The extracts below are taken from the preface, which is framed as a letter to her children.[4]

This letter shows the importance of making sure one's children are aware of the love between their parents. It also illustrates the truth that love for God ultimately must exceed love of the human beloved.

Lucy Hutchinson to her children

They who dote on moral excellencies, when by the inevitable
fate of all things frail, their adored idols are taken from them,
may let loose the winds of passion to bring in a flood of sorrow;
whose ebbing tides carry away the dear memory of what they
have lost; and when comfort is essayed to such mourners, com-
monly all objects are removed out of their view, which may with
their remembrance renew the grief; and in time these remedies
succeed, and oblivion's curtain is by degrees drawn over the dead
face, and things less lovely are liked, while they are not viewed
together with that which was most excellent. But I that am
under a command not to grieve at the common rate of a desolate
woman,[5] while I am studying which way to moderate my woe,
and if it were possible to augment my love, can for the present
find out none more just to your dear father nor consolatory to
myself than the preservation of his memory; which I need not
gild with such flattering commendations as the hired preachers
do equally give to the truly and titularly honourable. A naked,
undressed narrative, speaking the simple truth of him, will deck

him with more substantial glory, than all the panegyrics the best
pens could ever consecrate to the virtues of the best men. . . .

Let not excess of love and delight in the stream make us forget the fountain; he and all his excellencies came from God, and
flowed back into their own spring: there let us seek them, thither
let us hasten after him; there having found him, let us cease to
bewail among the dead that which is risen, or rather immortal.
His soul conversed with God so much when he was here, that
it rejoices to be now eternally freed from interruption in that
blessed exercise; his virtues were recorded in heaven's annals,
and can never perish; by them he yet teaches us and all those to
whose knowledge they shall arrive. It is only his fetters, his sins,
his infirmities, his diseases, that are dead never to revive again,
nor would we have them; they were his enemies and ours; by
faith in Christ he vanquished them. Our conjunction, if we had
any with him, was indissoluble; if we were knit together by one
spirit into one body of Christ, we are so still; if we were mutu-
ally united in one love of God, good men, and goodness, we are
so still. What is it then we wail in his remove? the distance?
Faithless fools! sorrow only makes it. Let us but ascend to God
in the holy joy for the great grace given his poor servant, and
he is there with us. He is only removed from the malice of his
enemies, for which, in being afflicted, we should not express our
love to him we may mourn for ourselves that we come so tardily
after him; that we want his guide and assistance in our way; and
yet if our tears did not put out our eyes we should see him even

*in heaven, holding forth his flaming lamp of virtuous examples
and precepts, to light us through the dark world. It is time that
I let in to your knowledge that splendour which, while it cheers
and enlightens your heavy senses, should make us remember to
give all his and all our glory to God alone, who is the father and
fountain of all light and excellence. . . .*

*For conjugal affection to his wife, it was such in him, as
whosoever would draw out a rule of honour, kindness, and
religion, to be practiced in that estate, need no more, but
exactly draw out his example; never man had a greater passion
for a woman, nor a more honourable esteem of a wife; yet he
was not uxorious, nor remitted he that just rule which it was
her honour to obey, but managed the reins of government with
such prudence and affection that she who would not delight in
such an honourable and advantageable subjection, must have
wanted a reasonable soul. He governed by persuasion, which
he never employed but to things honourable and profitable
for herself; he loved her soul and her honour more than her
outside, and yet he had even for her person a constant indul-
gence, exceeding the common temporary passions of the most
uxorious fools. If he esteemed her at a higher rate than she in
herself could have deserved, he was the author of that virtue
he doted on, while she only reflected his own glories upon him;
all that she was, was him, while he was here, and all that she
is now at best is but his pale shade. So liberal was he to her,
and of so generous a temper, that he hated the mention of*

*severed purses; his estate being so much at her disposal, that he
never would receive an account of anything she expended; so
constant was he in his love, that when she ceased to be young
and lovely, he showed most fondness; he loved her at such a
kind and generous rate as words cannot express; yet even this,
which was the highest love he or any man could have, was yet
bounded by a superior, he loved her in the Lord as his fellow-
creature, not his idol, but in such a manner as showed that an
affection, bounded in the just rules of duty, far exceeds every
way all the irregular passions in the world. He loved God
above her, and all the other dear pledges of his heart, and at
his command and for his glory cheerfully resigned them.*

Notes

1 The date of Lucy Hutchinson's death is unknown, though it had to have been
   after 1675.
2 Lucy Hutchinson, *Order and Disorder*, ed. David Norbrook (Oxford: Blackwell
   Publishers, 2001). The quotation is from ibid., xv.
3 Lucy Hutchinson, *Memoirs of the Life of Colonel Hutchinson*, ed. Julius
   Hutchinson (Repr. London: J.M. Dent & Sons, 1968), 370–371. Used by
   permission.
4 Ibid., 16–18, *passim*, and 24–25.
5 At the time of his death, Hutchinson had asked that Lucy be given this
   message: "Let her as she is above other women, show herself, in this occasion, a
   good Christian, and above the pitch of ordinary women." (Ibid., 379).

Chapter Four

PHILIP & MERCY DODDRIDGE

hilip Doddridge (1702–1751), a Londoner, was one of the most winsome writers of the eighteenth century. He had rich ancestral roots in Puritanism and his theological convictions were broadly Calvinistic. He is reckoned to have been something of a polymath, extremely competent in theology, mathematics, and physics.[1] In 1729, he accepted an invitation to be the minister of the Castle Hill Church in Northampton, which he pastored till his death in 1751. Here he wrote *The Rise and Progress of Religion in the Soul* (1745), which became a classic almost overnight and was instrumental in the conversion of William Wilberforce (1759–1833). A hundred years later, it had gone through numerous editions and had been translated into a number of languages, including Welsh, Scots Gaelic, Dutch, French, and Italian.

Doddridge was also "a great correspondent,"[2] and chief among his correspondents was his wife, Mercy, née Maris (1708–1790).[3] Doddridge wrote to her constantly when he was away from home. Their letters to one another were, in the words of Doddridge expert Geoffrey F. Nuttall, "often playful and always breathing the intimacy of a deep and unbroken mutual confidence," and, he added, were worthy of inclusion in "an anthology of such love letters."[4]

In these letters, we see how Christian lovers express their longing for one another's presence and how absence from one another can be mollified by the sharing of spiritual blessings.

Philip Doddridge to Mercy Doddridge[5]
Saturday night, Plymouth July 3, 1742

My dearest,

I am now at the greatest distance from you in person than I ever was, or I hope I ever shall be, for it is more than two hundred miles, yet I was never nearer to you in affection, and perhaps never more sensible of my happiness in being so near to you in relation.[6] *I have often thought of you this day, which has indeed been a very pleasant one, and pleasant days I would especially desire to share with you, indeed it is necessary I should so share them, in order to their being completely so. . . .*

Remember me to the dear children, and tell them I am very glad to hear they are so well, and that I pray for them every day. Their dear mamma may be sure she is not forgotten. I hope we shall have many comfortable days and Sabbaths together. And in the meantime, let us, whether present or absent from each other, own the divine goodness in preserving us so graciously thus long and endeavour to prepare more and more for that better world, where so many of our dear friends are awaiting us and where there will be no more absence. In the pleasant views of it, I am,

My dearest,
Your most affectionate,
—P. Doddridge

Philip Doddridge to Mercy Doddridge[7]
Northampton, October 31, 1742

My dearest,
I dispatched all the other letters which I had to write last night, but designedly reserved that which I intended for you till this morning, because I knew I might take the liberty of writing in a strain not ill-becoming a Sabbath, and a sacrament day;

nay, because I was sure my letter would be so much the more agreeable to you, in proportion to the degree in which it was suited to such a season. . . .

I hope, my dear, you will not be offended when I tell you that I am what I hardly thought it possible without a miracle, that I should have been very easy and happy without you. My days begin, pass, and end in pleasure, and seem short because they are so delightful. It may seem strange to say it, but really so it is. I hardly feel that I want anything. I often think of you, and pray for you, and bless God on your account, and please myself with the hope of many comfortable days and weeks and years with you. Yet I am not at all anxious about your return, or indeed about anything else. And the reason, the great suf-ficient reason, is that I have more of the presence of God with me than I remember ever to have enjoyed in any one month of my life. He enables me to live for him and to live with him. When I awake in the morning, which is always before it is light, I address myself to him and converse with him, speak to him while I am lighting my candle and putting on my clothes, and have often more delight before I come out of my chamber, though it be hardly a quarter of an hour after my awaking, than I have enjoyed for whole days or perhaps weeks of my life. He meets me in my study, in secret, in family devotions.[8] *It is pleasant to read, pleasant to compose, pleasant to converse with my friends at home; pleasant to visit those abroad—the*

*poor, the sick; pleasant to write letters of necessary business
by which any good can be done; pleasant to go out and preach
the gospel to poor souls, of which some are thirsting for it and
others dying without it; pleasant in the week day to think how
near another Sabbath is;—but, oh! much, much more pleasant, to think how near eternity is, and how short the journey
through this wilderness, and that it is but a step from earth to
heaven. . . .*

*The post calls, and I must therefore conclude, wishing
you all the happiness I feel, and more if your heart could
contain it.*

*My dearest, your ever affectionate friend,
Who hopes to love you forever,
—P. Doddridge*

Mercy Doddridge to Philip Doddridge[9]
Bath, November 7, 1742

My dear love,

*I heartily thank you for your delightful letter of October
31. I rejoice greatly in your sublime pleasures, nor at all wonder that such a degree of the divine presence should free your
mind from all anxious cares, and, in those serene moments,*

render you perfectly happy, and that independently of earthly friends. But I must confess that a part of your letter, delightful as it was, had a very different effect, and filled my mind with great anxiety and concern, and made me, indeed, as Miss Scott well expresses it, "almost tremble to think you are mortal." And this fear was increased much by a consciousness of the extreme tenderness my heart feels for you, which sometimes makes me dread lest I should sin you away, by giving you that place in my heart which ought to be sacred to God alone, next to whom I believe I am permitted to love you. Pray that I may rest there.

Nor was even this the only foundation of my concern, for I fear also lest these extraordinary manifestations of the divine favour, which lead you so ardently to thirst after souls, should engage you to labour beyond your strength, and so have a tendency to shorten life, dearer to me than anything in the world. . . .

I shall conclude, without further ceremony, by assuring you that I am, with all possible sincerity and tenderness, my dearest,

Entirely and affectionately yours,
—M. Doddridge

Philip Doddridge to Mercy Doddridge[10]
Northampton, November 13, 1742

My dearest,

    I could hardly believe my own eyes for joy last night when I saw your dear hand on the superscription of the letter I received from Bath, and then when I opened it and found four pages, with the delightful conclusion that you were still better, and had not had one bad symptom while writing, I cheerfully hope that God is answering our daily and affectionate prayers for you, and will restore you, ere many weeks are passed, in good health and spirits. Too much do I long for that happy time, and never did I find it more difficult to obey the calls of duty, in staying at home, than now that the better part of myself is at so great a distance. It signifies comparatively little to me who is, or who is not, at Bath, any farther than as your pleasure is concerned in their company. If you were in a cottage in the wilderness I had much rather, so far as this dear self of mine is concerned, be with you, than in the brightest, most polite, or most learned circle. And indeed the very reading of your letters is more to me than any other company or entertainment which books or friends can here afford me. . . .

                Your equally affectionate and faithful,
                    —Philip Doddridge

Philip Doddridge to Mercy Doddridge[11]
Northampton, March 3, 1743

My dearest,

*[Y]our last charming letter . . . came most seasonably,
and produced a very agreeable effect. You knew, my dearest,
it would arrive on Lord's day night. It was our sacrament day,
and, indeed, it was a most comfortable one to me. My joy at
that ordinance was so great that I could not well contain it.
I had much ado to forbear telling all about me, as well as I
could, for it would have been but in a very imperfect manner. What a Divine flame I felt in my soul, which, indeed, put
me greatly in mind of Mr. How[e]'s "full stream of rays."*[12]
*Were it possible to carry such impressions through life, it would
give the soul a kind of independence far too high for a mortal existence. It was, indeed, in the most literally and proper
sense, a "joy unspeakable, and full of glory!" I doubt not, my
dearest earthly friend, that it was, in a considerable measure,
in answer to your prayers. I had able measure, in answer to
your prayers. I had promised myself that we should then have
been together, but God was pleased to give me so much, that
he left no room to complain of what he withheld. You may be
assured, however, that I could not fail of remembering you in
such a circumstance. . . .*

I am, my Dearest, your own,

—P. Doddridge

Mercy Doddridge to Philip Doddridge[13]
Bath, March 12, 1743

My Dearest,

There is hardly any such thing as bearing your unparal-
leled generosity; and it is the daily joy and pleasure of my life to
recollect how greatly I am obliged to you, and above all, to the
Fountain of all my mercies, for giving me such a friend. I rejoice
in the divine goodness to you, and to me in you, that whilst you
are so constantly blessing and refreshing others, he is pleased to
return it so abundantly into your own bosom by favouring you
with such bright and extraordinary manifestations of his presence and grace. Much do I long to be with you, especially in
such happy seasons as these, in the humble hope to catch a little
of that sacred flame. It was no small disappointment to us to
be deprived of the great pleasure we had promised ourselves in
joining with you in that delightful ordinance, and enjoying your
valuable labours. And, indeed, my Sabbath was, I believe, in
some measure the less comfortable to me in consequence, for,
after all, instruments as well as ordinances are from above, and
God is pleased to bless your labours in a singular manner to my
edification and comfort. . . .

Did not Swift, my dearest, think you, prophesy of us when
he said, "it is seldom allowed to those persons who love one

another best to be much together."[14] *And this is, as he observes,*
to convince us of the imperfection of human happiness. Indeed,
I must freely own, this state of separation renders mine very
imperfect, notwithstanding all the advantages I might otherwise
boast of, as to society and friendship. . . .

[I]t is full time for me to conclude, and . . . I shall do so,
with wishing my dearest a good night, and assuring him that

> *I am, with all possible esteem and affection,*
> *most entirely his,*
> *—M. Doddridge*

Notes

1 D. L. Jeffery, "Doddridge, Philip," in *Biographical Dictionary of Evangelicals*, ed.
   Timothy Larsen (Leicester, England: Inter-Varsity Press/Downers Grove, Ill.:
   InterVarsity Press, 2003), 187.

2 Geoffrey F. Nuttall, "Doddridge's Life and Times," in his ed., *Philip Doddridge
   1702–1751: His Contribution to English Religion* (London: Independent Press,
   1951), 28.

3 On their marriage, see Malcolm Deacon, *Philip Doddridge of Northampton
   1702–51* (Northampton: Northamptonshire Libraries, 1980), 64–71.

4 Nuttall, "Doddridge's Life and Times," in *Philip Doddridge*, 29.

5 *The Correspondence and Diary of Philip Doddridge, D.D.*, ed. John Doddridge
   Humphreys (London: Henry Colburn and Richard Bentley, 1830), IV, 99–100.

6 Doddridge was on a preaching trip to Devon and the West Country of
   England.

7 *Correspondence and Diary of Philip Doddridge, D.D.*, IV, 123–126, *passim*.
   Mercy had gone to Bath to recover from a serious illness. See Deacon, *Philip
   Doddridge of Northampton*, 66.

8 For a comment on this text, see Nuttall, "Philip Doddridge—A Personal Appreciation," in *Philip Doddridge*, 158–159.

9 *Correspondence and Diary of Philip Doddridge, D.D.*, IV, 130–131, 133.

10 Ibid., IV, 139.

11 Ibid., IV, 211–212, *passim*.

12 This is a reference to the Puritan divine John Howe (1630–1705), one of Doddridge's favorite authors (Nuttall, "Philip Doddridge—A Personal Appreciation," in *Philip Doddridge*, 159–160). After Howe's death, an autobiographical passage was found in the frontispiece of his Bible. It noted that on one occasion, after Howe had realized that along with full intellectual assent to biblical truths there must be "a vivifying, savoury taste and relish of them," Howe had a dream that "a wonderful and copious stream of celestial rays, from the lofty throne of the Divine Majesty, did seem to dart into my open and expanded breast" (cited in Nuttall, "Philip Doddridge—A Personal Appreciation," in *Philip Doddridge*, 160).

13 *Correspondence and Diary of Philip Doddridge, D.D.*, IV, 215–216, 217, *passim*.

14 A quote from the Anglo-Irish satirist Jonathan Swift (1667–1745).

Chapter Five

BENJAMIN BEDDOME
& ANNE STEELE

he two leading Calvinistic Baptist hymn writers of the eighteenth century were, without a doubt, Benjamin Beddome (1717–1795), pastor from 1740 onward of the Baptist cause in Bourton-on-the-Water, Gloucestershire,[1] and Anne Steele (1717–1778), the daughter of the Hampshire Baptist pastor, farmer, and timber merchant William Steele (1689–1769). Their hymns were instrumental in the revitalization of the English Calvinistic Baptist community toward the close of the eighteenth century.

Beddome came to Bourton-on-the-Water in the spring of 1740. Over the next three years, he labored with great success

in the Bourton church. Significant for the shape of his future
ministry was a local revival that took place under his preaching in the early months of 1741, when around forty individuals were converted. At the time of Beddome's death in 1795,
almost his sole publication was a catechism he had drawn up
in the early 1750s. In the years that followed his death, however, a good number of his sermons were published, as was
a volume of 830 hymns. Nearly a hundred of these hymns
were still appearing in hymnals at the end of the nineteenth
century.

Although Anne Steele wrestled with ill health for much
of her life and never travelled far from her home in Hampshire, her hymns were highly treasured down to the beginning
of the twentieth century. In the opinion of her biographer, J.
R. Broome, no hymn writer has "excelled Anne Steele in her
tender, memorable, sensitive expression of the heart feelings
of a tempted, exercised, tried Christian."[2] Something of the
respect in which she and her hymns were held can be seen in
the fact that when she was dying, two of the leading Calvinistic Baptist ministers of the day, Caleb Evans (1737–1791) of
Bristol and the Londoner Samuel Stennett (1728–1795), came
to visit her.[3]

A few years ago, Broome discovered a letter among Steele's
papers in the archives of the Angus Library, Regent's Park
College, Oxford, that linked these two great hymn writers. It

appears that Beddome actually made a proposal of marriage on Dec. 23, 1742, that Anne rejected. Love's territory has its high points and low points, and rejected offers of love are not uncommon features on the map.[4] We have no record of Anne's reply, but it seems that Beddome's eloquence failed to persuade her. Beddome evidently recovered sufficiently from his disappointment to marry an Elizabeth Bothwell at a later date.

There also exists an exchange of letters between Anne and her half sister Mary, written in 1757 (when Anne was forty), which shows that Anne had at least one more proposal of marriage. When Anne wrote to tell her half sister that she had refused another proposal, Mary gave her a good telling off. Anne coolly replied that she was happy as she was, for marriage, in her opinion, came with many thorns. Indeed, when she looked into what she called the "meadow" of marriage, it was usually winter, she said. Mary responded that everyone else put up with the thorns, so why couldn't Anne? Besides, she rightly added, most people found that flowers grew on the thorns.

From a positive perspective, we see the way in which the hymnist Beddome makes use of poetry—in this case, that of John Milton (1608–1674)—to express his feelings—an excellent reminder of the role that poetry naturally plays in the communication of love.

Benjamin Beddome to Anne Steele [5]

Dear Miss

Pardon the Boldness which prompts me to lay these few lines at your feet. If continued thoughts of you and a disrelish to everything besides may be considered as arguments of love, surely I experience the passion. If the greatness of a person's love will make up for the want of wit, wealth and beauty, then may I humbly lay claim to your favour. Since I had the happiness of seeing you how often have I thought of Milton's beautiful description of Eve, book 8, line 471:

> . . . so lovely fair!
> That what seemed fair in all the world, seemed now
> Mean, or in her summed up, in her contained,
> And in her looks, which from that time infused
> Sweetness into my heart, unfelt before. . . . [6]

Madam, give me leave to tell you that these words speak the very experience of my soul, nor do I find it possible to forbear loving you. Would you but suffer me to come and lay before you those dictates of a confused mind which cannot be represented by a trembling hand and pen? Would you but permit me to cast myself at your feet and tell you how much I love you, what an easement might you thereby afford to a burdened spirit and at the same time give me an opportunity of declaring more fully that I am in sincerity,

> *Your devoted servant,*
> *—Benjamin Beddome*

Notes

1 On Beddome, see the extensive obituary written by John Rippon: "Rev.
  Benjamin Beddome, A.M. Bourton-on-the-Water, Gloucestershire," *Baptist
  Annual Register*, 2 (1794–1797), 314–326. This account was largely reproduced
  by Joseph Ivimey in *A History of the English Baptists* (London: Isaac Taylor
  Hinton/Holdsworth & Ball, 1830), IV, 461–469. For a significant biographical
  study from the nineteenth century, see also Thomas Brooks, *Pictures of the
  Past: The History of the Baptist Church, Bourton-on-the-Water* (London: Judd
  & Glass, 1861), 21–66. Very little has been written on Beddome during
  the past century, but see Derrick Holmes, "The Early Years (1655–1740) of
  Bourton-on-the-Water Dissenters who later constituted the Baptist Church,
  with special reference to the Ministry of the Reverend Benjamin Beddome
  A.M. 1740–1795" (unpublished certificate in education dissertation, St Paul's
  College, Cheltenham, 1969).
2 J. R. Broome, *A Bruised Reed: Anne Steele: Her Life and Times* (Harpenden,
  Hertfordshire: Gospel Standard Trust Publications, 2007), 175. This is the
  definitive life of Steele.
3 Ibid., 216.
4 For discussion of this letter, see ibid., 110–113.
5 Steele Papers STE 3/13 (Angus Library, Regent's Park College, University of
  Oxford). Used by permission.
6 *Paradise Lost*, 8.471–475 (John Milton, *Paradise Lost*, ed. John Leonard
  [London: Penguin, 2000], 179).

Chapter Six

HENRY & ELING VENN

enry Venn (1724–1797) received his tertiary education at Cambridge University, where he obtained
both his bachelor's and master's degrees and also became one of
the university's top cricketers. When he was ordained in June
1747, however, he stopped playing cricket as he did not want
to hear the cry from spectators, "Well played, Parson!"[1] Over
the next six years, he sought to be a conscientious and diligent
minister. However, he came to realize during 1752–1753 that
for his ministry to be in accord with the Scriptures, he needed
to rely not on the perfection of his obedience but "upon the all-
sufficient merits and infinite mercies of a Redeemer," namely
the Lord Jesus.[2]

In 1754, Venn became curate of Clapham, Surrey, where

he learned how to preach extemporaneously and where he became close friends of a number of prominent evangelicals, including George Whitefield (1714–1770) and Selina Hastings, the countess of Huntingdon (1707–1791). Marriage came in May 1757, when he was wedded to Eling Bishop, whose religious convictions and sweetness of temper made her an ideal wife and companion for Venn.[3]

A move to Huddersfield in 1759 was a great financial loss to Venn but a great spiritual gain to many in the parish. "A wilder people I never saw in England," John Wesley remarked about the people of this parish before Venn became their minister.[4] But before long, the church was filled with appreciative hearers of his sermons. In one three-year period during this time, there were some nine hundred conversions under Venn's preaching.[5]

The demands of this parish ministry eventually proved the undoing of Venn's health, and in 1771 he had to move to a small parish church at Yelling, twelve miles from Cambridge. His wife, though, did not make this move, for she had died in 1767. He married a second time in the year of his move to Yelling to a widow, Catherine Smith.

In an essay on Venn's spirituality, Bill Reimer has noted that his letters "exude a deep spirituality and an unwavering love for God."[6] The one below, written to Venn's first wife, Eling, when he was away on a preaching trip, is no exception.

True Christian love, like that of Henry Venn for his wife, ever seeks to direct the beloved's affections first of all to God. Far from diminishing the affection between the human lovers, such a Godward focus deepens it. Such is the paradox of love between the sexes when rightly placed in subordination to love for God.

To Eling Venn[7]
Nottingham, April 5, 1759

> *God has most graciously brought me, my dearest E., in increasing strength, to this town, within seventy miles of my journey's end; to perform which, I have before me two days and a half. I have been still highly favoured with the presence of our adorable Covenant God. This has cheered the way and made my time pass delightfully, though without company. Oh! how ought we to pray for those who live without God in the world! How forlorn their condition in many circumstances! How irksome to travel, as I shall, five or six hundred miles, a burden to themselves, if they turn their eyes inward; not able to have their own enjoyments, mean as they are, and no Invisible God, to hold sweet intercourse with by the way!*
>
> *Immediately upon my arrival here, I received your letter of good news, which was doubly acceptable, as I could not but be under many fears lest your concern for me might throw you back. How does our God abound in the most tender expressions of his favour towards us! How does he embrace us with mercy on every side!*

You will believe me, when I assure you, it gives me great plea-
sure to find you love me so tenderly. But you have need to beware,
lest I should stand in God's place; for your expressions, "that you
know not how to be from me an hour without feeling the loss,
etc." seem to imply something of this kind. My dearest E., we must
ever remember that word which God hath spoken from heaven:
"The time is short: let those who have wives be as if they had none;
and those who rejoice, as if they rejoiced not."⁸ Both for myself
and you, I would always pray that God may be so much dearer
to us than we are to each other that our souls in his love "delight
themselves in fatness,"⁹ and feel he is an all-sufficient God. By
this means we shall be most likely to continue together, and not
provoke the stroke of separation by an idolatrous love to one
another. By this means we shall love one another in God and for
God; and be armed with the whole armour of God for all events.

Write me word in your next—which you will direct to me
at Huddersfield—how you find the state of your immortal soul.
Surely God has abounded in loving-kindness to us more than to
others! Let us stir up each other to return sincere and vehement
love for all his benefits.

I can discover the horrible pride of my desperately wicked
heart in the disagreeable feeling the meanness of the towns I
pass through gives me, upon supposition I am to be fixed in one
like them. What deep root have worldly lusts in my soul! And
how easy it is to have the name of having overcome the world,
yea, to flatter ourselves we really have done it by faith, when

still love to comfortable accommodations and to have things handsome about us prevails.

Dinner is just coming upon table. I have also to see my horse fed. And therefore, without filling the other side,[10] I must conclude, praying that the Eternal God may be your refuge, the redemption which is in Jesus your portion, and the Holy Ghost your comforter. Grace be with you, and all in our house!

—*H. Venn*

Notes

1 Leonard W. Cowie, "Venn, Henry," in *Oxford Dictionary of National Biography*, eds. H. C. G. Matthew and Brian Harrison (Oxford: Oxford University Press, 2004), 56:253.

2 John Venn, "Memoir [of Henry Venn]," in *The Letters of Henry Venn*, ed. Henry Venn, Jr. (1836 ed.; repr. Edinburgh/Carlisle, Pa.: Banner of Truth Trust, 1993), 21.

3 Ibid., 25–26.

4 Cowie, "Venn, Henry," in *Oxford Dictionary of National Biography*, 56:254.

5 W. J. Clyde Ervine, "Venn, Henry," in *The Blackwell Dictionary of Evangelical Biography 1730–1860*, ed. Donald M. Lewis (Oxford/Cambridge, Mass.: Blackwell, 1995), II, 1137.

6 Bill Reimer, "The Spirituality of Henry Venn," *Churchman*, 114 (2000) (available online at www.churchsociety.org/churchman/documents/Cman_114_4_Reimer.pdf; accessed Sept. 16, 2008).

7 From *Letters of Henry Venn*, 72–74.

8 See 1 Corinthians 7:29–30.

9 Cf. Isaiah 55:2.

10 A reference to writing on the other side of the letter.

Chapter Seven

THOMAS & SALLY CHARLES

he Welsh Calvinistic Methodist Thomas Charles (1755–1814) was educated at Llanddowror and a Dissenting academy at Carmarthen.[1] While at the academy, he happened to visit Llangeitho, where he was converted under the preaching of the remarkable Daniel Rowland (1713–1790). He went up to study at Jesus College, Oxford, from 1775 to 1778, and during this time he made the acquaintance of a number of evangelicals, including John Newton (1725–1807) and William Romaine (1714–1795). After his graduation from Jesus College, he became a curate in Somerset and was ordained as a priest in the Church of England in 1780.

Two years prior to this, though, he had met Sally Jones (1753–1814), a shopkeeper's daughter in Bala, North Wales, and fallen in love with her. Although she did not reciprocate his affections at first, as one of the letters below reveals, he persisted in seeking her hand in marriage until they were finally wed on Aug. 20, 1783.

Because of his leanings toward the Calvinistic Methodist movement, Charles was dismissed from a Church of England parish near Bala in 1784. He proceeded to make Bala a center for Calvinistic Methodism and, when the Calvinistic Methodists reluctantly seceded from the Church of England en masse in 1811, Charles was their leader. He also played a key role in the development of the Sunday school movement in Wales and in the establishment of the British and Foreign Bible Society.[2]

The love letters between Thomas and Sally, written throughout their married lives, provide a tremendous picture of what a Christian marriage should look like. The kind of forthright honesty Sally demonstrated with her future husband at the beginning of their relationship is essential to any strong Christian marriage. Honesty and transparency, however, are vital not only for the start of a relationship but for its continuance and growth. These letters also reveal how love is rooted in friendship. One's spouse must be one's best friend.

Thomas Charles to Sally Jones[3]
Queen Camel, December 28, 1779

My very dear friend,

Such an unexpected address from a person who never saw you but once, and that at such a long interval of time, will I suppose at first not a little surprise you. However I flatter myself that thus circumstanced it comes with the more recommendation, when I assure you that long as the interval is since I had the pleasure of seeing you, you have not been absent from my mind for a whole day, from that time to this.

The first report of your character (which I heard at Carmarthen by some of our religious friends about six years ago) left such an impression on my mind as, I am sure, no length of time can ever obliterate. I immediately conceived an ardent desire, and a secret hope, that my Heavenly Father's wise and good Providence would so order subsequent events that I should in due time see that beloved person of whom I had formed such a favourable opinion.

When Mr. Lloyd[4] gave me a kind invitation to spend part of the summer with him at Bala, 'tis inexpressible what secret pleasure and joy the prospect of seeing you afforded me. Nor was I disappointed. The sight of so much good sense, beauty and unaffected modesty, joined with that genuine piety which eminently adorns your person, administered fuel to the fire already enkindled, and which has continued burning with increasing ardour from that time to this. I should then have explained to you what this letter informs you of, had not difficulties (then insurmountable) been in the way, originating from circumstances which I hope at some future period you'll give me leave to acquaint you with.

Ever since I came to England I have anxiously expected (and not without some foundation, as assured by my friends) that some favourable circumstance would open a door for my return to Wales (a place forever dear!), but hitherto I have been disappointed. Finding that any longer delay would serve only to distract my mind, and by constant uneasiness in some degree, unfit me for the proper discharge of that very important office in which I am engaged, I determined upon the resolution, which I now put in execution, of writing to you, and solicit the favour of a correspondence with you, till such time as kind Providence indulges us with an interview, which on my part is most ardently desired. . . .

Be perfectly assured that nothing but real regard and sincere affection for your person only could ever induce me to write or speak to you on such a subject. You are the only person that ever I saw (and the first I ever addressed on the subject), with whom I thought I could spend my life in happy union and felicity, and for whom I possessed that particular affection and esteem requisite for conjugal happiness; and you are the only temporal blessing I have for some time past asked with importunity of the Lord.

I hope that your determination will happily convince me that the Lord's answer is favourable. I shall be present with you when you peruse this, how anxious I shall be for your determination; 'tis impossible to tell how happy would I deem myself, could I be really present then to confirm to your full satisfaction what I assert in this letter! But as that at present is impossible, I hope to commit this, as well as all other events to him, who rules supremely in the whole universe, and orders all things in the best manner for the advancement of his own glory, and the eternal welfare of his people, and no doubt will order this even for our mutual happiness. To whose mercy and protection I shall not fail to recommend you by constant prayers, and intercessions for you, which are never more ardent and sincere than when you are interested in them.

I shall anxiously wait for a letter from you. I hope it will be favourable. Communicate your thoughts with freedom, and without the least reserve, for you may depend with unshaken confidence upon the most inviolable secrecy from me, if required, as to anything you shall please to communicate. . . . [Farewell,] my dearest friend. Pray for me, and believe me, [I am,] with the most sincere and invariable affection,

Your most unfeigned friend and humble servant,
—Thomas Charles

Sally Jones to Thomas Charles[5]
Bala, January 17, 1780

Reverend Sir,

Your letter doth indeed seem something strange to me. I can neither give it full credit nor throw it aside heedless. May he who knoweth your motive in writing, give me simplicity to answer and let the consequence be what it will.

The liberty and privilege of my present state are very dear and valuable to me. I often wish I had no temptation to part with them; but I can't say I have ever determined or known the will of God concerning it. I trust his providence will in time make this clear. I have several reasons that I do not choose to engage in a correspondence of this nature. But if any letters be exchanged between us I would wish each of us should have free liberty to drop the correspondence at pleasure.

Probably after receiving this you will not wish to write again. This will be no disappointment to me. I quit my claim of every profession in your letter excepting one, which is the remembrance of me at the throne of mercy. This is a pleasing thought which I am willing to cherish, and though I do not expect to see you in this vale of troubles, yet I shall meet you where I hope my gratitude will be in full perfection, there to express it to the glory of him that heareth the prayer of his people for one another and blesses them in the remotest part of the earth.

I have by your permission shown your letter to my father.[6]
He and my mother join in cordial respects and love to you. I
believe my poor father is an Israelite indeed in whom there is no
guile.[7] *He, dearest of mortals, thinks everything sincere. I join*
with him in best wishes for your prosperity in the glorious and
very weighty work you are engaged,

Who am your well-wisher,
—Sally Jones

Pray let a candid eye pass over my scroll. I have wrote in some
hurry.

Thomas Charles to Sally Jones[8]
Queen Camel, March 1, 1780

My dearest friend,
Though my head aches, and hand trembles (being a little
indisposed this week past), yet I sit down with the greatest
pleasure to write a few lines in answer to your last favour, and
not without the intention of extorting if possible (with whatever
"reluctance you may go about it"[9]*) another in return. It is a*
great relief to my mind to write to you at all, but I set about it
with redoubled pleasure, when I entertain the fond hope of its
inducing you to write to me. "As cold waters to a thirsty soul,
so is good news to me from a far country."[10] *So that you see I*

*have no intention, nor can I bear the thoughts of "dropping our
correspondence."*[11]

*It is impossible for me not to think of you, and you know
what satisfaction and relief it affords the mind, when it dwells
long on any object to communicate its thoughts. Besides, you
cannot but suppose, if you think I am in the least degree sincere
in what I say, it will be to the highest degree pleasing for me
to hear from you, were it but to be informed that you are well
and that heaven smiles upon you. If you are unwilling that
our correspondence should be known and talked of amongst
our Bala friends (which I infer to be the case from an expression in your letter), though I regard not its being known to the
whole universe, yet to satisfy you I would direct my letters to
Mr. Foulks*[12] *and you could have yours directed by him to me.
I would approve of anything but dropping our correspondence.
This I really cannot think of. And I hope you will look upon it
in a different point of view when you write to me (which I hope
will be soon) next, from what you did in your last.*

*Your observation is very just that "our happiness doth not
consist in anything transitory."*[13] *No, there can be no happiness but in the enjoyment of the inexhaustible and overflowing
source of all goodness and perfection. As we lost our happiness
by separating ourselves from God, so the only way of regaining
it is, by returning to him again: for he has promised to meet us
in Christ and there (and nowhere else) to be forever reconciled
to us. But notwithstanding, creatures, not "as they are subject*

to vanity,"[14] but as creatures of God can, and do, contribute much to our happiness by his (observe) blessing. God has diffused himself through all his creatures, and when we enjoy him in his creatures, then they answer to us the end for which they were created; so that the love of God and of his creatures not only are consistent, but inseparably connected together.

For this reason so much stress is laid in Scripture upon our loving Christ's true disciples, our Christian brethren, as a sure infallible sign of our loving the children of God. God has more highly and wonderfully honoured, and put infinitely more value upon a true believer (however mean in the eyes of the world, and despised by it) than any, or all, of his other creatures put together. And God's perfections are more illustriously manifested in him than in all his other works. How is it possible then for any that love God to hate him who is so unspeakably dear to God, and in whom so much of God is to be seen? It cannot be. As God hath loved his children here in dust and ashes, with a love superior to that which he bears to all his other creatures (a love so amazing and wonderful as to stagger our belief by its greatness!), in the same manner does one Christian love another. He loves him next to the Almighty.

Hence, as you observe, Christian friendship is certainly "the best we can wish to commence," though "not the only one I desire to know,"[15] but a friendship by no means repugnant to it, but grounded upon that. For I assure you, were all the perfections of your sex united in you, and the wealth of the Indies in *your possession, and I had not reason to believe you were an adopted child of our Heavenly Father, and belonging to God's family, by the help of God's grace I should hope never to desire forming any connection with you. But as I know it to be the happy case with you, it is my most earnest desire and ardent prayer to God I may succeed. And I know I shall, if for his glory, and our mutual benefit and happiness.*

I feelingly sympathize with you when you inform me that "the thoughts of death are alarming to you."[16] *It was the case with me for many sorrowful years. But, through the abundant goodness of my Heavenly Father, it is not generally the case with me at present. That Scripture, 1 Cor. 15:25, 26, was very remarkably blessed to me for the removing of all the very alarming and anxious thoughts about death which till then deprived me of lasting comfort. Death is considered there not so much our enemy as Christ's, and he must reign till he hath put all enemies under his feet; and though death will be the last enemy, yet death must be destroyed.*

I saw I had nothing to do but enjoy the victory, Christ is engaged to conquer. The victory is obtained by the arm of omnipotence, and we shall, ere long, bear the palm in our hands as a token of it. Till that happy time arrives may it be our constant care and study to live in the fear and to the glory of him who hath thus loved us, and vanquished our strong enemies for us.

O! it is pleasing, it is comfortable, to view Christ in the field of battle, bearing the weak believer on his shoulder, through whole legions of hellish foes, to the blessed mansions in his Father's house. Not one of them shall be lost. His Father and our Father is greater than all and none shall pluck one of his sheep out of his hand.[17] *O, what a Saviour! O, what a salvation hath God provided for us! Shall we not praise him! Yes, I hope you and I shall join our songs through the boundless period of eternity, and praising God and the Lamb! 'Tis all we can render to him for his marvelous loving–kindness.*

I sincerely thank you for your remembrance of me at the throne of grace. You never can do me a greater kindness, though you have it in your power to oblige more than any person on earth. God hath promised to hear our prayers: "ask and ye shall have" is His unlimited promise.[18]

With an aching head and trembling hand you find I have been able to write a very long letter to you. I shall not ask pardon for its length, but desire you to imitate my example. I am just on the point of removing from my present situation,[19] *but whatever changes and revolutions I may experience, my heart will forever remain the same towards you. There no change can affect me, but shall always be able with the greatest sincerity, to subscribe myself,*

Dearest of mortals!

Your most affectionate friend and humble servant,

—Thomas Charles

———

Sally Jones to Thomas Charles[20]
Bala, April 27, 1780

Reverend Sir,

*I retire from business and attempt to answer your letter.
O, that retiring from the world were retiring from an evil
heart. I would then have some grateful feelings to join with
yours in praises to him whom my soul desireth to love. But
I fear to offer strange fire. I can better talk of lukewarm-
ness, deadness and disaffection. These are qualities purely
my own. I do not glory in them, but willing to lose them in
that love which Paul could not fathom.*[21] *O, may the cheer-
ing, warming influence of the Sun of righteousness dissolve
the hardness of my heart!*[22] *I believe nothing else can do it. A
view of redeeming love, Jesus dying on the cross, is the most
powerful quickening. If that fails, farewell life and happiness
anywhere else. O, may my fruitless complaints never be permitted to dishonour him! I would lay the fault where it ought
to be. The straightness is here; in Jesus there is all fullness—
—another Saviour I do not wish.*

I am glad you are settled to your satisfaction.[23] *It is no
small privilege to be among them who fear the Lord. "As iron
sharpeneth iron, so doth the face of man his friend."*[24] *It is
happy that the success of your labour doth not depend on*

the tenderness of natural dispositions, but on the power and faithfulness of God who hath not deceived his people (who are commissioned by him to preach the gospel to all creatures) with a promise that he will be with them[25] *without giving them some fruit of their labour, or rather the fruit of his sufferings. May you be more and more alienated to your carnal brethren. Their favours kill more than their frowns. Since it hath been my lot to converse with you of these things, I can't but wish your prosperity. . . .*

I hope you will let no consideration of honour keep up our correspondence because it hath begun, but whenever you have satisfaction to drop it, do it with freedom. If I am not greatly deceived in myself, this will be the most satisfactory proof I can have that the thing is not from the Lord. The freedom I use in writing to you doth not proceed from a slavish passion. I trust my esteem will keep apace with the working of Providence, whatever that will be.

My father and mother join in love to you. My father is troubled with the headache today. We are not apprehensive of the least danger. He is subject to it some time. He has given me some droll commands for you, but my paper is short and my fingers almost frozen. They are nothing worth inserting. So farewell.

—Sally Jones

Thomas Charles to Sally Jones[26]
Milborne Port, November 18, 1780

My dear dearest heart,

To be persuaded that I possess a place in your affection and esteem affords me more real satisfaction than anything of a temporal nature possibly could, or, I am certain, ever can; not because I vainly suppose that I deserve, in any degree, a place there, but because I sincerely love you, my dearest love, and wish for a place therein. And I am still more satisfied that this regard proceeds not so much from blind passion as from clear conviction. Passions are unsteady things: they are no sooner excited but they subside again and cannot be depended upon, but what proceeds from conviction is likely to be lasting. Passions are blind and dangerous leaders, but when they faithfully follow conviction they preserve their proper place and are not amiss. . . .

My sure source of comfort is that your heart is at his disposal who can do nothing that is either wrong in itself, or prejudicial to the real interest of any of his children. To his hands I can, through grace, with joy commit all my cares and concerns.

I can, with the utmost consistency, with truth, make the same profession. Whatever influence passion now may have over my mind, I am certain my regard for you at first originated more from conviction than from passion. Nor have I for one single moment any the least suspicion that my affections are wrong placed; but conviction of their being placed on a proper object keeps my mind steady without shadow of alteration. The sight and the thought of every other person that I ever heard of only make me love you the more. Never anything occurs that has the least tendency to effect a change in the bent of my mind in this respect; but I do, my sweet love, beyond expression love you.

Whilst I am expressing the present state of my mind towards you, I would not willingly, at the same time, forget to say something that may have, by the blessing of God, a tendency to establish your faith in and increase your love towards him to whom we are under such infinite obligations as will forever challenge and distance all returns. What returns can we ever make for Christ, the gift (what a gift!) of the Father? The very thought confounds and oppresses the mind! What returns can we make the Son of God "for his agony and bloody sweat, his cross and passion"[27]? Poor creatures! We can do nothing but with amazement forever stand and gaze and wonder at the height and depth of his love, and confess that none but God could show such love. . . .

It comforts my soul that you remember me at the throne of grace. Continue to pray for me. I cannot forget you whilst able to remember myself. "May the Lord of all consolation fill you with all joy in believing."[28]

> *Farewell my sweet love.*
> *I am your own,*
> *—Thomas Charles*

Thomas Charles to Sally Jones[29]
Milborne Port, November 25, 1780

My sweet love,

. . . Few days ago I received a letter from a Mr. [John] Newton, one of the most eminently pious gospel ministers now in England, with whom when at the University I spent three months one summer; in which letter is the following curious passage, which, lest I should forget to show on some future opportunity, I cannot help here transcribing. He himself has been married for many years, but is not the language different from that of the married in general?

I understand you have marriage in view. The Lord I trust has shown you the right person. May he bring you happily together and bless the connection. It is a weighty business, but when put under the management of faith, prayer and prudence, it is a happy business. A day which will have a powerful influence upon every future day and circumstance of life, may be truly deemed important. Such is the wedding day. However I shall be glad to hear you are enrolled in the honourable rank of husbands.

It always pleases me to hear that a minister is well married. There is something in domestic life that seems suited to improve our meetness for speaking to our people. The growing soul when doubled in wedlock, and multiplied in children, acquires a thousand new feelings and sensibilities of which the solitary bachelor is incapable, and these teach and dispose us to feel for others, and give us interest both in their pleasures and their pains. And this sympathizing temper is a happy talent for a minister to possess. It will give him a deeper place in the hearts of his people, than some more shining accomplishments.[30]

This language pleases me. How happy shall I be, my sweet love, when able to inform him that you are mine! Till then I must be contented to be the solitary bachelor and as such a stranger to a thousand pleasing feelings and sensations. Continue to express your good will towards me and I shall not be totally devoid of happiness even now and every returning sun will shine more bright till that happy day arrives.

If you knew the feelings of my mind you would think this no exaggeration, nor would you be backward to believe that your letters are good for the headache. I did not say that they were good for headaches in general, but that they are more efficacious to cure my headache than all the drugs of the apothecaries' shops. Happy experience gives me no room to doubt.

I do love you, my sweet dear, and whilst I feel this pleasing painful passion, I cannot be easy or happy but as I hear of your welfare and happiness. When the time comes for me to hear from you, if disappointed one post, a multitude of distressing thoughts continually haunt me, nor am I able by any means to rid myself of them. My friends, however I may attempt to mask *myself, instantly perceive the alteration, nor are they at a loss for the cause of it; and they all smile and are happy when the lawyer's letter (so they call yours, from your hand) is received. Such is the real state of my mind at present respecting you, but I hope it will not long continue so.*

With my sweet love!
Yours beyond expression,
—Thomas Charles

Notes

1 For Charles' life, see especially the definitive three-volume biography by D. E. Jenkins, *The Life of the Rev. Thomas Charles, B.A., of Bala* (Denbigh: Llewelyn Jenkins, 1908).

2 For the letters that follow, I am deeply grateful to Dr. E. Wyn James, senior lecturer and co-director of the Cardiff Centre for Welsh American Studies, School of Welsh, Cardiff University, who is preparing an edition of the letters of Thomas and Sally Charles to each other. Dr. James selected and edited the letters included here. I am responsible for their annotation.

3 From Jenkins, *The Life of the Rev. Thomas Charles*, I:146–148.

4 Simon Lloyd was a fellow Oxford student who had invited Charles to visit him in Bala during the summer of 1778.

5 From the *Journal of the Historical Society of the Presbyterian Church of Wales*, 31:2 (June 1946), 39.

6 Thomas Foulk(e)s (1731–1802), Sally's stepfather. He was a convert of John Wesley (1703–1791).

7 Cf. John 1:47.

8 From Jenkins, *The Life of the Rev. Thomas Charles*, I:156–158.

9 Charles is quoting from a letter written to him by Sally on Feb. 14, 1780.

10 Cf. Proverbs 25:25.

11 Another quotation from Sally's letter to Charles on Feb. 14, 1780.

12 Sally's stepfather, Thomas Foulk(e)s.

13 Another quotation from Sally's letter to Charles on Feb. 14, 1780.

14 Cf. Romans 8:20.

15 More quotations from Sally's letter to Charles on Feb. 14, 1780.

16 Another quotation from Sally's letter to Charles on Feb. 14, 1780.

17 Cf. John 14:2; 17:12; 10:28.

18 Cf. Luke 11:9.

19 Charles moved to Milborne Port on March 27, 1780.

20 From Jenkins, *The Life of the Rev. Thomas Charles*, I:171–172.

21 Cf. Ephesians 3:19.

22 Cf. Malachi 4:2.

23 Charles had moved to Milborne Port on March 27, 1780.

24 Cf. Proverbs 27:17.

25 Cf. Mark 16:15; Matthew 28:20.

26 From Jenkins, *The Life of the Rev. Thomas Charles*, I:225–227; Edward Morgan, *Thomas Charles' Spiritual Counsels* (Edinburgh: Banner of Truth Trust, 1993), 235–237.

27 This phrase was a common homiletical description of the work of the Lord Jesus.

28 Cf. Romans 15:13.

29 From Jenkins, *The Life of the Rev. Thomas Charles*, I:227–229.

30 John Newton (1725–1807) was one of the most important evangelical authors and ministers of the eighteenth century. This extract is from a letter to Charles dated Nov. 21, 1780. The manuscript is in AL 322, the Porteus Library, University of London. This very extract from the letter appears in Edward Morgan, A *Brief History of the Life and Labours of the Rev. T. Charles, A.B., Late of Bala, Merionethshire* (London: Hamilton, Seeley, Hatchard, Jones, Hughes, 1828), 76–77. For all of the information about this extract, I am indebted to Marylynn Rouse of Stratford-upon-Avon, England, and her expertise with regard to the life and writings of Newton.

Chapter Eight

SAMUEL & SARAH PEARCE

amuel Pearce (1766–1799) was born in Plymouth into a sturdy Baptist home.[1] He was converted in the summer of 1782 and baptized the following year. The Baptist work at Plymouth soon recognized that God had gifted him for vocational ministry. Accordingly, he was given opportunities to use his gifts in small-group settings in Plymouth. In 1786, he went to study at Bristol Baptist Academy, the only institution in Britain for the training of men for the Baptist ministry. He was there for three years, graduating in 1789. That year he began his one and only ministry, at Cannon Street Baptist Church in Birmingham, a town that was mushrooming under the impact of the Industrial Revolution. He had an extremely fruitful ministry till his death in 1799. He was also vitally involved in the formation of the Baptist Missionary Society in 1792 and was a close friend and correspondent of missionary William Carey (1761–1834).

A vital support to Pearce throughout his pastorate at Cannon Street was his closest friend, his wife, Sarah. A third-generation Baptist,[2] Sarah Hopkins (1771–1804) had met Pearce soon after his arrival in Birmingham. Pearce was soon deeply in love with Sarah, and she with him. He wrote to her on Dec. 24, 1790, about the impact her letters had on him: "Were I averse to writing . . . one of your dear Epistles could not fail of conquering the antipathy and transforming it into desire. The moment I peruse a line from my Sarah, I am inspired at the propensity which never leaves me, till I have thrown open my whole heart, and returned a copy of it to the dear being who long since compelled it to a *voluntary surrender*, and whose claims have never since been disputed."[3] They were married on Feb. 2, 1791.

Pearce expressed his understanding of what should lie at the heart of their marriage in a letter he wrote to his future wife a little over two months before their wedding: "May my dear Sarah & myself be made the means of leading each other on in the way to the heavenly kingdom & at last there meet to know what even temporary separation means no more."[4] For Pearce, husbands and wives were to be a means of grace to one another in their earthly pilgrimage. In other words, they were to be "intimate allies."[5] In fact, after Pearce's early death in 1799 from tuberculosis, one of Sarah's friends commented to her that she was blessed to have enjoyed "so intimate a union with such an uncommon man."[6]

In the letters Samuel wrote to his wife, we see how he continued to stir up her love for him after their marriage. The pursuit of the beloved does not end with the marriage ceremony. Also evident in these letters is the way in which Samuel comforted his wife in their trials, a model for believers today.

———

Samuel Pearce to Sarah Pearce [7]
Northampton, December 13, 1794

My dear Sarah,

I am just brought on the wings of celestial mercy safe to my Sabbath's station. I am well, and my dear friends here seem healthy and happy; but I feel for you. I long to know how our dear Louisa's pulse beats; I fear still feverish. [8] *We must not, however, suffer ourselves to be infected with a mental fever on this account. Is she ill? It is right. Is she very ill . . . dying? It is still right. Is she gone to join the heavenly choristers? It is all right, notwithstanding our repining. . . . Repinings! No; we will not repine. It is best she should go. It is best for her; this we must allow. It is best for us; do we expect it? Oh what poor, ungrateful, shortsighted worms are we! Let us submit, my Sarah, till we come to heaven; if we do not then see that it is best, let us then complain.*

But why do I attempt to console? Perhaps an indulgent providence has ere now dissipated your fears; or if that same kind providence has removed our babe, you have consolation enough in him who suffered more than we; and more than enough to quiet all our passions in that astonishing consideration, "God so loved the world, that he spared not his own Son."[9] *Did God cheerfully give the holy child Jesus for us; and shall we refuse our child to him? He gave his Son to suffer; He takes our children to enjoy. Yes; to enjoy Himself.*

Yours with the tenderest regard,
—S.P.

Samuel Pearce to Sarah Pearce[10]
[London, September 7, 1795]

. . . Every day improves not only my tenderness but my esteem for you. Called as I now am to mingle much with society in all its orders I have daily opportunity of making remarks on human temper and after all I have seen and thought my judgment as well as my affection still approves of you as the best of women for me. We have been too long united by conjugal ties to admit a suspicion of flattery in our correspondence or conversation. . . . I begin to count the days which I hope will bring me to a re-enjoyment of your dear company.

Samuel Pearce to Sarah Pearce[11]
Dublin June 24, 1796

. . . For my part, I compare our present correspondence to a kind of courtship, rendered sweeter than what usually bears that name by a certainty of success and a knowledge of the suitableness of my dear intended. Not less than when I sought your hand, so I now covet your heart, nor doth the security of possessing you at all lessen any pleasure at the prospect of calling you my own, when we meet again the other side of St. George's Channel.[12] . . . O our dear fireside! When shall we sit down toe to toe, and tête-à-tête again. Not a long time I hope will elapse ere I reenjoy that felicity.

Sarah Pearce to Mrs. Franklin[13]
Alcester, July 11, 1800

After an illness of a few days, it hath pleased the great Arbiter of life and death to bereave me of my dear little boy, aged one year and six months, and thus again to convince me of the uncertainty of all earthly joys and bring to remembrance my past sorrows. He was in my fond eyes one of the fairest flowers human nature ever exhibited; but ah, he is dropt at an early period! Yet the hope

of his being transplanted into a more salutary clime, there to
re-bloom in everlasting vigour, and the reflection that if he had
lived, he had unavoidably been exposed to innumerable tempta-
tions, from which if my life was spared, I should yet be unable to
screen him, make me still. Though I feel as a parent and I hope
as a Christian, yet I can resign him.

Oh could I feel but half the resignation respecting the loss
of my beloved Pearce! But I cannot. Still bleeds the deep, deep
wound; and a return to Birmingham[14] is a return to the most
poignant feelings. I wish however to resign him to the hand that
gave and that had an unquestionable right to take away. Be
still then every tumultuous passion, and know that he who hath
inflicted these repeated strokes is God: that God whom I desire
to reverence under every painful dispensation, being persuaded
that what I know not now, I shall know hereafter.

Notes

1 On Pearce, see S. Pearce Carey, *Samuel Pearce, M.A., The Baptist Brainerd* (3rd
   ed.; London: The Carey Press, n.d.), and Michael A. G. Haykin, "Calvinistic
   Piety illustrated: A study of the piety of Samuel Pearce on the bicentennial of
   the death of his wife Sarah," *Eusebeia*, 2 (Spring 2004), 5–27. A selection of his
   letters is forthcoming: Michael A. G. Haykin, *"Joy unspeakable and full of glory":
   The Piety of Samuel & Sarah Pearce* (Grand Rapids: Reformation Heritage
   Books, 2008).

2 Her father was Joshua Hopkins (d. 1798), a grocer and a deacon in Alcester
   Baptist Church, Warwickshire, for close to thirty years. Her maternal
   grandfather was John Ash (1724–1779), pastor of the Baptist cause in Pershore,
   Worcestershire, and a noteworthy Baptist minister of the eighteenth century.

3 Letter to Sarah Hopkins, Dec. 24, 1790 (Pearce-Carey Correspondence 1790–1828, Angus Library, Regent's Park College, University of Oxford).

4 Letter to Sarah Hopkins, Nov. 26, 1790 (Samuel Pearce Carey Collection—Pearce Family Letters, Angus Library, Regent's Park College, University of Oxford).

5 For this phrase I am indebted to the title of a book on marriage by Dan Allender and Tremper Longman III: *Intimate Allies* (Carol Stream, Ill.: Tyndale House, 1995).

6 R. Franklin, letter to Sarah Pearce, Nov. 23, 1800 (Samuel Pearce Mss. [Angus Library, Regent's Park College, University of Oxford]).

7 From *Andrew Fuller, Memoirs of the Rev. Samuel Pearce, A.M.* (3rd ed.; Dunstable: J. W. Morris, 1808), 80–81.

8 Louisa Pearce, their daughter, was ill. She would die in 1810.

9 John 3:16; Romans 8:32.

10 Samuel Pearce Mss. Used by permission. After the formation of the Baptist Missionary Society, Pearce played a key role in raising funds for the mission, which meant long trips from home.

11 Ibid. Used by permission. Samuel was on a preaching mission to Ireland.

12 That is, the Irish Sea.

13 From [Andrew Fuller,] "Memoir of Mrs. Pearce," *The Theological and Biblical Magazine*, 5 (1805), 3. This letter was written when the Pearces' youngest child, Samuel, died. Mrs. Franklin lived in Coventry. See ibid., 2, n* She was probably the wife of Francis Franklin (ca. 1773–1852), a Bristol alumnus and the pastor of the Cow Lane Baptist Chapel, Coventry, from 1798 to 1852.

14 This letter was written from Alcester, which is not far from Birmingham, in the year after Pearce's death.

Chapter Nine

—◆◆

ADONIRAM & ANN JUDSON

*O*f all the lands where English-speaking Christians have sought to plant churches, Burma, now known as Myanmar, has turned out to be one of the most fruitful. Undoubtedly the central figures in the church-planting endeavor in Burma were the Judsons, Adoniram (1788–1850) and his courageous wife, Ann (1789–1826).[1] When one considers their labors and incredible trials in that far eastern land, the patience they showed in the six years that passed before they saw the first convert, Moung Nau, their careful translation of the Scriptures into Burmese—a translation that is still the standard version—it is no surprise that the lives of the Judsons have been an inspiration to uncounted Christians for the past century and a half.[2]

Adoniram Judson was born Aug. 9, 1788, in Malden, Massachusetts. Although he was raised in a Christian home, his latter teen years were spent in rejecting his parents' faith. He had gone to study at Brown University in Rhode Island, where he imbibed Deism and became absorbed by the pursuit of fame. The death of Jacob Eames, the young man who had introduced him to Deism, shook Judson deeply and brought him to an intellectual commitment to Christianity. In October 1808, he entered the Andover Theological Seminary in Massachusetts, and the following month he "began to entertain a hope of having received the regenerating influences of the Holy Spirit."[3] Along with a few other divinity students at Andover, he was soon gripped by the need to take the gospel to other nations, and in the fall of 1811 he was appointed a missionary by the newly formed Congregationalist mission society. He would sail the following year to India, and from there he would journey on to Burma. At the end of his life, there were close to eight thousand Burmese believers gathered in sixty-three churches.[4]

Travelling with him was a new wife, Ann, née Hasseltine. He had met her in June 1810, and exactly two years later they were married and landed at Calcutta.

The two letters that follow were written before their marriage. The first is Judson's extraordinary letter to Ann's father, requesting his permission to wed Ann.[5] The shared sense of a common mission that characterizes these letters should mark every Christian marriage, for all Christians are servants of God where he has planted them. Spouses should keep this mission before one another and encourage one another in it. It is all too common for spouses to live much of their lives together in separate worlds.

Adoniram Judson to John Hasseltine
[Summer, 1810]

> . . . I have now to ask whether you can consent to part with your daughter early next spring, to see her no more in this world? Whether you can consent to see her departure to a heathen land, and her subjection to the hardships and sufferings of a missionary life? Whether you can consent to her exposure to the dangers of the ocean; to the fatal influence of the southern climate of India; to every kind of want and distress; to degradation, insult, persecution, and perhaps a violent death? Can you consent to all this, for the sake of perishing immortal souls; for the sake of Zion and the glory of God? Can you consent to all this, in hope of soon meeting your daughter in the world of glory, with a crown of righteousness brightened by the acclamations of praise which shall redound to her Saviour from heathens saved, through her means, from eternal woe and despair?

Adoniram Judson to Ann Hasseltine
January 1, 1811. Tuesday Morning

*It is with the utmost sincerity, and with my whole heart, that
I wish you, my love, a happy new year. May it be a year in
which your walk will be close with God; your frame calm and
serene; and the road that leads you to the Lamb marked with
purer light. May it be a year in which you will have more
largely the Spirit of Christ, be raised above sublunary things,
and be willing to be disposed of in this world just as God shall
please. As every moment of the year will bring you nearer the
end of your pilgrimage, may it bring you nearer to God, and
find you more prepared to hail the messenger of death as a
deliverer and a friend. And now, since I have begun to wish,
I will go on.*

*May this be the year in which you will change your
name; in which you will take final leave of your relatives
and native land; in which you will cross the wide ocean, and
dwell on the other side of the world, among a heathen people. What a great change will this year probably effect in our
lives! How very different will be our situation and employ-
ment!! If our lives are preserved and our attempt prospered,
we shall next new year's day be in India, and perhaps wish*

each other a happy new year in the uncouth dialect of Hin-
dostan or Burma. We shall no more see our kind friends
round us, or enjoy the conveniences of civilized life, or go to
the house of God with those that keep holy day; but swarthy
countenances will everywhere meet our eye, the jargon of an
unknown tongue will assail our ears, and we shall witness the
assembling of heathen to celebrate the worship of idol gods.
We shall be weary of the world, and wish for wings like a
dove, that we may fly away and be at rest. We shall probably
experience seasons when we shall be "exceeding sorrowful,
even unto death."[8] We shall see many dreary, disconsolate
hours, and feel a sinking of spirits, anguish of mind, of
which now we can form little conception. O, we shall wish
to lie down and die. And that time may soon come. One of
us may be unable to sustain the heat of the climate and the
change of habits; and the other may say, with literal truth,
over the grave:

> By foreign hands the dying eyes were closed;
> By foreign hands thy decent limbs composed;
> By foreign hands thy humble grave adorned.[9]

But whether we shall be honored and mourned by strang-
ers, God only knows. At least, either of us will be certain of one
mourner. In view of such scenes shall we not pray with earnest-
ness, "O for an overcoming faith," etc. ?[10]

Notes

1 For Judson, see especially Courtney Anderson, *To the Golden Shore: The Life of Adoniram Judson* (Boston/Toronto: Little, Brown and Co., 1956).

2 This paragraph is taken from Michael A. G. Haykin, "Foreword" to Sharon James, *My Heart in His Hands: Ann Judson of Burma: a life with selections from her Memoir and letters* (Darlington, Co. Durham: Evangelical Press, 1998), 9.

3 Adoniram Judson, "Autobiographical Record of Dates and Events," in Edward Judson, *Adoniram Judson, D.D.* (London: Hodder and Stoughton, 1883), 562.

4 K. P. Mobley, "Judson, Adoniram, Jr.," in *Biographical Dictionary of Evangelicals*, ed. Timothy Larsen (Leicester, England: Inter-Varsity Press/Downers Grove, Ill.: InterVarsity Press, 2003), 339.

5 After Ann's death in 1826, Judson married two more times and outlived both of those wives.

6 From Judson, *Adoniram Judson, D.D.*, 20. John Hasseltine was Ann's father.

7 Ibid., 20–21.

8 See Mark 14:34.

9 These lines are from Alexander Pope, *Elegy to the Memory of an Unfortunate Lady*, lines 51–53.

10 This is the first line of a hymn by Isaac Watts (1674–1748).

Chapter Ten

JOHN & LOTTIE BROADUS

ohn Albert Broadus (1827–1895), a Virginian, was converted in 1843, but was unsure of his calling for three years or so. This time of indecision came to a close when he entered the University of Virginia in 1846 and committed himself to preparing for pastoral ministry. At the university, he excelled as a student, and after graduation in 1850 he was called the following year to pastor Charlottesville Baptist Church. The year of his graduation was also significant in that he married Maria Carter Harrison (d. 1857), the daughter of Gessner Harrison, his Greek professor at the university.

Broadus served the Charlottesville congregation until 1859, at which time he accepted an invitation from his close friend

James Petigru Boyce (1827–1888) to join the founding faculty of The Southern Baptist Theological Seminary. Boyce served as the school's first president and professor of theology, while Broadus taught New Testament and homiletics. Originally located in Greenville, South Carolina, the seminary had to shut its doors during the American Civil War (1861–1865), when Broadus served as a chaplain in the Army of Northern Virginia, which was commanded by Robert E. Lee (1807–1870). Southern reopened after the war, but as David Dockery has noted, Boyce could not have succeeded in rebuilding the school if it had not been especially for Broadus and another founding faculty member, Basil Manly, Jr. (1825–1892).[1] It was Broadus who once uttered the famous words that characterized the determined spirit of the founders of Southern: "The seminary may die, but let us die first."[2] After Boyce's death in 1889, Broadus became the second president of the seminary.

After the death of his first wife, Broadus had married Charlotte Eleanor Sinclair, whom he called Lottie. Perusal of a significant number of letters to her from Broadus and she to him over the course of their marriage reveals two Christians who took great delight in one another, missed each other deeply when duty called Broadus to be away—either during the war or while seeking to promote the seminary after the war—and who knew the importance of a Christian marriage.

One thing the other letters in this small anthology

have shown, but which these letters reveal very keenly, is the writer's unguarded admission of his or her need for the beloved. Such frank openness is often lacking in our age of self-sufficiency. The final letter of Broadus is also of note, for it models the way in which Christian spouses should ask one another's forgiveness.

Lottie Broadus to John Broadus[3]
June 8, 1861

O! to think of it—you are at Ch[arlottes]ville now while I write—and seeing so many dear, dear, friends. I do hope that you enjoy it, and are improving in health. Do not hurry home too soon on my account. I am so anxious that you should be benefited, that I'm willing for you to stay away any length of time it may require for that.

How I thank you for taking so much pains to write to me everything so far as you had gone. . . . Nothing else in the whole world could give me half so much pleasure. . . .

Good-bye my precious husband—it is now late Saturday evening. To-morrow you will, I am thinking, preach in your own old church at Charlottesville. Love to my friends. Your devoted wife,

—Lottie

Lottie Broadus to John Broadus [4]
June 11, 1861

My dear husband

I am just from the prayer-meeting—and now at this hour (10 p.m.) there is nobody awake with me, and what can I think of, but of you, and how help, longing to have you here with me. But O! the sweet comfort that you love me, far away as you are; and you may be at this moment thinking of, perhaps praying for, your wife. . . .

With all the love my heart can give,

—Lottie

John Broadus to Lottie Broadus [5]
Wednesday, September 2, 1863

My dearest Lottie,

. . . Lottie, it is possible—of course it is—that I may not see you anymore. Four weeks, four weeks and I may have ceased to breathe. So I'll tell you right now, here in the still night, in the room where at this hour we have often fallen asleep together, in the house where I first won your timid consent to be my bride, that I love you more now than ever before, more and more every year of the five—that I love you as much as I ever loved any other, or ever could have learned to love anyone that lives.

*Lottie, won't you love me too—don't you? Won't you pour
all the wealth of your woman's love, undoubting, without any
reserve, into my bosom, and let it flood my soul with sweetness? Won't you unlock every recess of your heart, and let all
its affections rush forth in one rich, full tide of love? Won't
you forgive [me] if I have sometimes been exacting, apparently
neglectful—won't you forget that you have ever yielded to one
moment's skepticism about my love—won't you just surrender
your whole heart to trustful and joyful affection for your lover
and your husband?*

*True, I am a man of bare ambition, with fondly cherished
hopes of doing some good, and of gaining the good opinion of
men, but O my darling, the life of my life is bound up in your
love. Tell me, tell me, that without reserve, from a full, overflowing heart, you love me—that you will always love me, with
your whole heart—and I am happy, and there is nothing earth
can give or take away that shall render me really unhappy—for
are we not both trying, amid all our weakness, to trust in the yet
loftier and richer love of our God and Saviour? Then love me,
Lottie, love me—see how much more you can love me—I claim
to deserve it only on one ground, that I love you—love me,
dearest, love me, love me, love me, love me.*

*I am unwilling to cease writing. I want to keep begging
you to love me. Not that I doubt you, dearest—O no!—fond,
faithful, true, self-sacrificing, devoted wife—gentle, tender,
sweetheart wife—I know you love me dearly, and for that very*

reason I want you to love me more, dearest, more. But while I
write, I feel not so far distant; and when I stop, the wires seem
to be cut, and the blank, impassable space stretches out between
us. Lottie, won't you love me?

> Ever tenderly yours,
> —John A. Broadus

John Broadus to Lottie Broadus[6]
Covington, June 15, 1874

My dear wife,

Thank you for writing to me—only sorry for the effort I
know it cost you to write so long a letter. I am grieved & pained
that my failure to consult you last winter should have seemed to
you a slight and an unkindness. You have so often shown, about
my going to the army, going to Europe,[7] etc., the "heroism" you
should speak of so ironically, that seeing this year's work to be
the crisis of my life, I took for granted your concurrence.

I could not read your letter without distress. Yet it is a comfort to see that though displeased with me, you love me. Please
love me always, through thick and thin. Please believe that
though I am often very unwise, though I seem to you unkind,
I do heartily and tenderly love you. There are many wiser and
kinder husbands, but no man loves his wife better than I do.

I have felt at a loss what to do and have decided the best I could. If Boyce had not published appointments, I should go home immediately. But it would be a terrible damper on his efforts if I should fail to keep the appointments. I cannot forget that Boyce got me my house, Boyce sent me to Europe, and this that I am doing now is not merely work for the Seminary, but a personal help and kindness to him. Boyce has undertaken to make this collection in K[entuck]y, and wants my help, needs it. But he has never urged me, has always said I must do what I think I can.

I conclude to stay in K[entuck]y (unless special sickness of yourself or the children should require . . . [me] to go sooner) till latter part of July, and then go home and stay there. During August, if we live, I shall be at your service. . . . Make Sam say lessons in Latin & Greek to Lida, and read history, for occupation. When I get home, I'll try to take things in hand.

I preached twice yesterday without suffering inconvenience. Slept well, am in good health, and could improve and enjoy myself if I were not every hour distressed about you.

Brethren waiting for me now.

Your own loving husband,
[John A. Broadus]

Notes

1 David S. Dockery, "Mighty in the Scriptures: John A. Broadus and His Influence on A.T. Robertson and Southern Baptist Life," in *John A. Broadus: A Living Legacy*, eds. David S. Dockery and Roger D. Duke (Studies in Baptist Life and Thought; Nashville: B&H Publishing Group, 2008), 18. This collection of essays by Dockery and Duke is the best contemporary study of Broadus. See also Craig C. Christina, "Broadus and the Establishment of The Southern Baptist Theological Seminary," in ibid., 122–155.

2 Dockery, "Mighty in the Scriptures," in ibid., 20.

3 From the John Albert Broadus Collection, Box 1, Folder 54 (Archives of the James P. Boyce Centennial Library, The Southern Baptist Theological Seminary, Louisville, Ky.). Used by permission. For help with these letters from the Broadus collection, I am indebted to Jason Fowler, archivist, and his staff.

4 Ibid. Used by permission.

5 Ibid. Used by permission.

6 In the Mitchell Family Papers (Archives of the James P. Boyce Centennial Library, The Southern Baptist Theological Seminary, Louisville, Ky.). Used by permission.

7 In 1870, Broadus had been given an all-expenses-paid trip to Europe by the seminary. See Christina, "Broadus and the Establishment of The Southern Baptist Theological Seminary," in *John A. Broadus*, 139.

Chapter Eleven

MARTYN & BETHAN LLOYD-JONES

David Martyn Lloyd-Jones (1899–1981) was born in Cardiff, Wales, although he spent most of his youth in Llangeitho and London.[1] His earliest experiences of church life were in the Presbyterian Church of Wales, heir to the evangelical theology and fervent piety of Calvinistic Methodism, of which Thomas Charles had been a major architect. Sadly, by Lloyd-Jones' day, the evangelical fervor and spirituality of the denomination had largely fallen prey to liberal theology and attempts to effect social betterment through education and political action.

In his early teens, his family moved to London. There, during the momentous days of World War I, Lloyd-Jones

enrolled as a student at the medical school of St. Bartholom-
ew's Hospital. After graduation in 1921, he worked closely for
three years with the physician to the royal family, Sir Thomas
(later Lord) Horder (1871–1955). But despite the prospect of
a dazzling career in medicine, Lloyd-Jones began to have serious doubts about continuing as a doctor. He became convinced
that the root problem of many of his and Horder's patients was
spiritual. Their spiritual state, though, brought to the fore his
own personal need of a relationship with God through Christ.

Lloyd-Jones' conversion, which he never dated, took place
at some point in 1923 or 1924. Attending it was a call and a
passion to preach the gospel in his native Wales. Lloyd-Jones
never had any formal theological training, though he was an
assiduous student of the Scriptures, theology, and church history. His pastoral gifts were recognized at the end of 1926,
when he received a call to pastor Bethlehem Forward Movement Mission, a Calvinistic Methodist work in Sandfields,
Aberavon. A few weeks later, on Jan. 8, 1927, he married
Bethan Phillips, whom he had loved for at least nine years
prior to their marriage. Martyn and Bethan had a singularly
happy marriage. According to their grandson, Christopher
Catherwood, they "complemented each other and were able to
strengthen each other" throughout their long lives together.[2]

At the close of the 1930s, Lloyd-Jones left Aberavon
for Westminster Chapel, London, to serve as the associate of
G. Campbell Morgan (1863–1945). World War II scattered

most of the large congregation that had delighted in Morgan's preaching. Thus, when the war was over, Lloyd-Jones had to rebuild the congregation from around one hundred or two hundred. By the 1950s, attendance was often close to two thousand. These people were drawn by the clarity of biblical exposition, the spiritual power, and the doctrinal depth of Lloyd-Jones' preaching.

Lloyd-Jones retired in 1968 and died thirteen years later. His final days were typical of the man. Dying of cancer, he had lost the power of speech. On Thursday evening, Feb. 26, 1981, he wrote a note for Bethan and their family: "Do not pray for healing. Do not hold me back from the glory."[3]

Lloyd-Jones had one of the richest and most important ministries of the twentieth century, but this letter reveals how vital a role his wife played in that ministry. Bethan was a key support to her husband throughout their lives together, as every husband or wife should be to his or her spouse.

Martyn Lloyd-Jones to Bethan Lloyd-Jones[4]
25 September, 1939

My dear Bethan,

Thank you for your letter of this morning, though I am very angry that you should have been up till 11.30 p.m. writing it! I see that you are quite incorrigible![5] The idea that I shall become used to being without you is really funny. I could speak for a long time on the subject. As I have told you many, many times, the passing of the years does nothing but deepen and intensify my love for you. When I think of those days in London in 1925 and '26, when I thought that no greater love was possible, I could laugh. But honestly, during this last year I had come to believe that it was not possible for a man to love his wife more than I loved you. And yet I see that there is no end to love, and that it is still true that "absence makes the heart grow fonder." I am quite certain that there is no lover, anywhere, writing to his girl who is quite as mad about her as I am. Indeed I pity those lovers who are not married. Well, I had better put a curb on things or I shall spend the night writing to you without a word of news. . . .

Ever yours,
—Martyn

Notes

1 For studies of Lloyd-Jones' life, see Iain H. Murray, *David Martyn Lloyd-Jones* (Edinburgh: Banner of Truth Trust, 1982 and 1990), 2 vols.; Christopher Catherwood, "Martyn Lloyd-Jones," in his *Five Evangelical Leaders* (London: Hodder and Stoughton, 1984), 51–109; and J. I. Packer, "David Martyn Lloyd-Jones," in *Chosen Vessels: Portraits of Ten Outstanding Christian Men*, ed. Charles Turner (Ann Arbor, Mich.: Servant Publications, 1985), 108–123.

2 Catherwood, *Five Evangelical Leaders*, 57.

3 Murray, *David Martyn Lloyd-Jones*, 2:747–748.

4 From D. Martyn Lloyd-Jones, *Letters 1919–1981*, selected by Iain H. Murray (Edinburgh: Banner of Truth Trust, 1994), 47. Used with permission.

5 Apparently Bethan did not believe in going to bed early.

Chapter Twelve

HELMUTH & FREYA VON MOLTKE

ount Helmuth James von Moltke (1907–1945), the son of a German aristocrat and his South African wife, read law at university.[1] He then worked in various law firms and eventually completed his legal training in England. He had met his future wife, Freya, née Deichmann, the daughter of a prominent banker, in the summer of 1929. Two years later, amid major financial difficulties for both families, they married.

In 1939, when World War II began, Moltke was drafted to work in the Nazi regime's counterintelligence agency. As a devout Christian and an opponent of Adolf Hitler (1889–1945), however, Moltke used his position to save prisoners and hostages. He came to see that only a person who believed in God could be a total opponent of the Nazi government. He expected the defeat of Germany and thus drew up plans for a postwar German democracy.

Moltke was personally opposed to the use of violence against the Nazi regime, as he believed that would make the perpetrators little better than the Nazis. Nevertheless, he was linked to the attempt to overthrow Hitler. On Jan. 19, 1944, Moltke was arrested for warning someone who was in danger of arrest. He was tried in the People's Court by Roland Freisler (1893–1945) and hanged in Plötzensee Prison in Berlin on Jan. 23, 1945.

This letter to Freya, one of sixteen hundred that Moltke wrote to her during the course of their love and marriage, presents a strong picture of the oneness of Christian marriage and how, in the words of the Song of Solomon, "many waters cannot quench love," for it is stronger than death (Song 8:7, ESV).

Helmuth von Moltke to Freya von Moltke
Tegel, January 10, 1945

My dear,
    I must first say quite decidedly, that the closing hours of a man's life are no different from any others. I had always

*imagined that one would have no feeling beyond shock, and
that one would keep saying to oneself, "This is the last time
you'll see the sun go down, this is the last time you'll go to bed,
you've only got twice more to hear the clock strike twelve." But
there is no question of any of that. Perhaps I'm a little above
myself, I don't know, but I cannot deny that I feel in the best of
spirits at the moment. I can only pray to our Heavenly Father
that he will keep me thus, since to die so is obviously easier for
the flesh. How good God has been to me! I must risk sound-
ing hysterical, but I'm so filled with gratitude that there's really
room for nothing else. His guidance of me was so sure and clear
during those two days. Had the whole court been in uproar, had
Herr Freisler and the surrounding walls tottered before my eyes,
it would have made no difference to me. I felt exactly as it says
in Isaiah, chapter 43, verse 2: "When thou passest through the
waters, I will be with thee: when thou walkest through the fire,
thou shalt not be burned; neither shall the flame kindle upon
thee," . . . that is to say upon thy soul.*

*Now there remains but a short, hard way before me, and
I can only pray that God will continue as good to me as he has
been hitherto. . . . Yesterday, my dear, we read this beautiful
passage: "But we have this treasure in earthen vessels, that the
excellency of the power may be of God, and not of us. We are
troubled on every side, yet not distressed; we are perplexed but
not in despair; persecuted, but not forsaken; cast down, but
not destroyed; always bearing about in the body the dying of*

the Lord Jesus, that the life of Jesus might be made manifest
in our body."³ Thanks be, my dear, before all things to God.
Thanks also to your dear self, for your intercessions, and
thanks to all those who have prayed for us and me. That I,
your husband, weak, cowardly, "complicated," very ordinary
though I be, should have been allowed to experience this! Were
I now to be reprieved—which I swear is no more and no less
likely than it was a week ago—I must admit that I should have
my way to find all over again, so tremendous has been the
demonstration of God's presence and mighty power. He shows
us these and shows them quite unmistakably, precisely when he
deals with us as we ourselves should not choose. . . . There is
only one thing, my dear, that I can say: May God be as good to
you as he has been to me, then even the death of your husband
will not count. God can show himself all-powerful at any
time, whether you are making pancakes for the boys or whether
you are looking after their little insides. I ought to say good-
bye to you—but I cannot. I ought to deplore and lament all
your humdrum daily toil. I cannot. I ought to think of all the
burdens which now fall on your shoulders, but I cannot. There
is only one thing which I can say: if you keep the consciousness
of absolute sincerity when the Lord gives it to you—a security
which you would never have known if it had not been for this
time and its issue—then I shall leave behind me as my legacy a
treasure which none can confiscate, against which even my life
cannot weigh in the balance. . . .

I will write again tomorrow, but since one cannot tell what will happen I want to have touched on all subjects in my letter. Of course I do not know whether I shall be put to death tomorrow. It may be that there will be a further hearing, perhaps I shall be beaten or put in store. Try to get in touch with me, for that may perhaps preserve me from too fierce a beating. Although I know after today's experience that God can turn to naught this beating too—even if I have no whole bone in my body before I am hanged—although therefore at the moment I do not fear it, yet I should prefer to avoid it. So Good-night, be strong and of a good courage.

———

January 11, 1945

My dear, I want to chat with you for a little while. . . .

In a hymn there occur the lines: "Then he for death is ready, who living clings to Thee." That is precisely how I feel. Today, since I am alive, I must "living cling to Him." More than that he does not ask. Is that Pharisaic? I do not know. But I think I know that I am living only in his grace and for-giveness. I have nothing which I derive from myself, there is nothing which I can do of myself. . . . The following, as it turned out, was the really dramatic thing about the trial. During the proceedings all factual charges had proved to be untenable, and were dropped. Finally nothing was left but this (which, however, struck such terror into the Third Reich that it had to condemn five men—ultimately the number will be seven—to death). It was established that a private individual, namely myself, had discussed with two ecclesiastics, both of them Protestants, with a Provincial of the Jesuits, and with a number of bishops, matters "which are the exclusive concern of the Führer"—and all this without the smallest intention of taking any active steps (this too was established). The discussions had embraced no questions of organization or the construction of the Reich. All suggestion of that fell away during the course of the proceedings, and Schulze,[4] in his summing-up, expressly stated that this case "differs radically from all parallel cases, for in the conversations there was no mention of violence or organized opposition"—whereas the question under discussion was the demands in practice of the Christian ethic, nothing more. And it is for that alone that we stand condemned.

Freisler said to me in the course of one of his tirades: "Only in one respect does the National Socialism resemble Christianity: we demand the whole man." I don't know whether the others sitting there took it all in, for it was a sort of dialogue between Freisler and me—a dialogue of the spirit, since I did not get the chance to say much—in the course of which we got to know one another through and through. Freisler was the only one of the whole gang who thoroughly understood me, and the only one of them who realized why he must do away with me. . . . In my case it was all grimmest earnest. "From whom do you take your orders, from the other world or from Adolf Hitler? Where lie your loyalty and your faith?" . . .

The decisive phrase in the proceedings was, "Herr Count, Christianity has one thing in common with us National Socialists, and one thing only: we claim the whole man." I wonder whether he really understands what he said there. Just think how wonderfully God has moulded this, his unworthy vessel. . . . I was and still am innocent of all connection with the use of violence. . . . Then he humbled me as I have never been humbled before, so that I learnt to pray for his forgiveness and to trust myself to his grace. Then he brought me here, so that I may see you standing fast, which means that I can be free of thoughts of you and the boys—that is to say, of worry about you. He gave me time and opportunity to settle everything that can be settled, so that all earthly cares may fall away. Then he let me taste in all their bitterness the agony of parting, the terror of death, and the fear of hell, so that these are also behind me. Then he endows me with faith, hope and charity, and with such full measure that it is really overwhelming. . . . I stood before Freisler not as a Protestant, not as a great landowner, not as a noble, not as a Prussian, not as a German even. . . . No, I stood there as a Christian and as nothing else. . . .

That I should have been chosen to undertake so mighty a task! All the pains God has taken with me, the intricate twists and turns of conduct, the everlasting tacking, the purport of it all was suddenly revealed within an hour on January 10, 1945. . . .

And now my dear, I come to you. I have not included you in my list because you, my dear, stand in a totally different position from all the others. You are not one of God's agents to make me what I am, rather you are myself. You are my thirteenth chapter of the First Epistle to the Corinthians. Without this chapter no human being is truly human. Without you I would have accepted love. . . . But without you, my dear, I would not have "had" love. I should not think of saying that I love you; that would be quite false. Rather you are the one part of me, which would be lacking if I was alone. . . . It is only in our union—you and I—that we form a complete human being. . . . And that is why, my dear, I am quite certain that you will never lose me on this earth—no, not for a moment. And this fact it was given us to symbolize finally through our common participation in the Holy Communion, that celebration which was my last.

I wept a little, not that I was sad, not that I was dispirited, not that I wanted to turn back—no, I wept for gratitude, because I was overwhelmed by this proof of the presence of God. True, we cannot see him face to face but we cannot be overmastered, when we suddenly realize that a whole lifetime through he has gone before us as a cloud by day and as fire by night and that he lets us see that suddenly in a moment. . . .

Since God has the unbelievable goodness to be in me, I can take with me not only you and the boys but all those whom I love and numberless others who are not so near to me. You can tell them that.

*My dear, my life draws to its close, and I can truthfully
say of myself, "He died in the fullness of years and of life's
experience." That does not imply that I would not gladly go
on living, that I would not gladly walk further at your side on
this earth. But for that I should need a new commission from
God since the one for which he created me stands completed. If
he has another commission for me, then it will be made clear
to us. Therefore go steadily ahead with your efforts to save my
life, in case I should survive this day. Perhaps after all, he will
set me another commission.*

*I will stop, since there is no more to say. I have not named
any whom I would have you greet or salute for me, since you
know well whom my affections embrace. All the texts that we
both love are enshrined in my heart, as they are in yours. But
I would end by saying to you from the depths of my being and
from the fullness of that treasure wherewith he hath filled this
humble earthen vessel,*

> "The grace of our Lord Jesus Christ, and the
> love of God, and the fellowship of the holy
> Ghost, be with you all evermore. Amen."[5]

Notes

1 For his life, see Michael Balfour and Julian Frisby, *Helmuth von Moltke: A Leader Against Hitler* (London: Macmillan, 1972).

2 From *A German of the Resistance: The Last Letters of Count Helmuth James von Moltke* (2nd ed.; London: Oxford University Press, 1948), 41–52, *passim*. Used by permission.

3 2 Corinthians 4:7–10.

4 A German official who read out the indictment against Moltke at his trial.

5 2 Corinthians 13:14.

FOR FURTHER READING

*W*hen it comes to Christian wisdom about love and marriage, the Puritans cannot be bettered. See, in this regard, J. I. Packer, "Marriage and Family in Puritan Thought," in his *A Quest for Godliness: The Puritan Vision of the Christian Life* (Wheaton, Ill.: Crossway, 1990). For a superb Puritan treatment, see the relevant pages in Richard Baxter, *The Christian Directory* (Grand Rapids: Reformation Heritage Books, 2008).

For an excellent analysis of three eighteenth-century marriages—those of John and Molly Wesley, George and Elizabeth Whitefield, and Jonathan and Sarah Edwards—along with some practical application—see Doreen Moore, *Good Christians, Good Husbands? Leaving a Legacy in Marriage & Ministry* (Fearn, Ross-shire: Christian Focus, 2004).

For studies of the biblical material about marriage, see especially Geoffrey W. Bromiley, *God and Marriage* (Grand Rapids: Eerdmans, 1980); Daniel L. Akin, *God on Sex: The*

Creator's Ideas about Love, Intimacy and Marriage (Nashville: Broadman & Holman, 2003); and John Piper, *This Momentary Marriage: A Parable of Permanence* (Wheaton, Ill.: Crossway, 2009). Dan B. Allender and Tremper Longman III, *Intimate Allies* (Wheaton, Ill.: Tyndale, 1995), is also a tremendously helpful and practical study.

ABOUT THE AUTHOR

Dr. Michael A. G. Haykin is professor of church history and biblical spirituality at The Southern Baptist Theological Seminary in Louisville, Ky., where he also serves as director of the Andrew Fuller Center for Baptist Studies.

Dr. Haykin earned his B.A. in philosophy from the University of Toronto and his M.Rel. and Th.D. from Wycliffe College at the University of Toronto.

He is the author of numerous books, including *One heart and one soul: John Sutcliff of Olney, his friends, and his times* (Evangelical Press, 1994); *'At the Pure Fountain of Thy Word': Andrew Fuller as an Apologist* (Paternoster Press, 2004); *Jonathan Edwards: The Holy Spirit in Revival* (Evangelical Press, 2005); and most recently, *The God who draws near: An introduction to biblical spirituality* (Evangelical Press, 2007).

Dr. Haykin and his wife, Alison, and their two children, Victoria and Nigel, live in Dundas, Ontario. They attend Trinity Baptist Church, Burlington, Ontario, where he and his wife are members and where he has served as an elder.

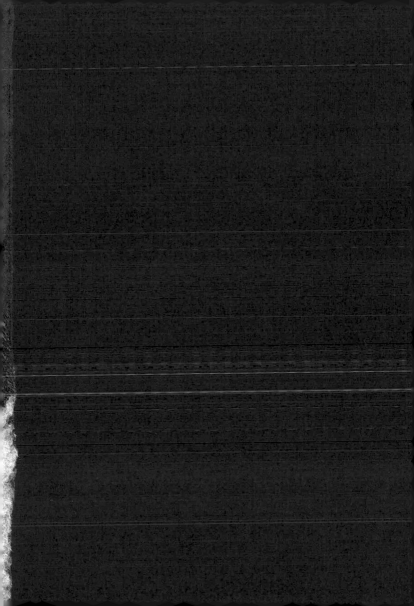